TOP 10 MEXICO CITY

CONTENTS

4 Introducing Mexico City

18 Top 10 Highlights

50

Top 10 of Everything

82

Area by Area

120

Streetsmart

MEXICO CITY

INTRODUCING

Basílica de Santa María de Guadalupe

WELCOME TO

MEXICO CITY

Big, bold, buzzy: dynamic Mexico City is just as comfortable honoring its history and traditions as it is at setting trends in contemporary art and architecture, food and fashion. Don't want to miss a thing? With Top 10 Mexico City, you'll enjoy the very best the city has to offer.

Described as "the capital of the 21st century" by journalist and author David Lida, Mexico City exists on a grand scale. Its central plaza, the Zócalo, is fronted by the majestic Catedral Metropolitana and the city's vast Palacio Nacional; once the main ceremonial site of the Aztecs, the square today hosts the country's most important events. There are more museums here than in any city in the world bar Paris, covering every conceivable interest – and some inconceivable ones, too. When the city's residents want a bucolic break, they head for leafy

Daily street life in Mexico City

Bosque de Chapultepec, the largest urban park in Latin America, which is itself home to the biggest museum in the country, the Museo Nacional de Antropología.

But look beyond the superlatives and you'll find a city of more understated charms, a place of courtyard cafés and street-corner taco stands, bijou art galleries and old-fashioned perfume shops, secret gardens and late-night jazz joints. Venture beyond the Centro Histórico to explore the city's diverse neighborhoods, each with its own unique history and atmosphere: upscale Polanco, with its fine-dining restaurants; tranquil San Ángel; or artsy Coyoacán, where the Museo Frida Kahlo offers an intimate insight into Mexico's most famous artist. And while the capital could keep you busy for a lifetime, it's also the perfect jumping-off point for a variety of day trips, taking in colorful nearby towns, ancient pyramids, Aztec remains, and a picturesque national park that's dominated by a pair of brooding volcanoes.

So, where to start? With Top 10 Mexico City, of course. This pocket-sized guide gets to the heart of the city with simple lists of 10, expert local knowledge, and comprehensive maps, helping you turn an ordinary trip into an extraordinary one.

THE STORY OF MEXICO CITY

From capital of the Aztec empire to global metropolis: in many ways, Mexico City has always been a sprawling, teeming urban center. Throughout the centuries, it has witnessed revolutions, celebrations, and natural disasters. Here's the story of how it came to be.

Mexico City Begins

The valley where Mexico City sits today was occupied from the first century CE, but it wasn't until 1325 that the Aztecs established their capital, Tenochtitlán, here. They set about expanding the settlement, gradually constructing a great city that included pyramids, palaces, public buildings, and a ceremonial center. It is reckoned that this was one of the three largest cities on earth by the time Europeans arrived.

In November 1519, Spanish colonizer Hernán Cortés and his troops first laid eyes on Tenochtitlán and were overawed by the city they saw before them. Initially, the Spaniards were welcomed by Aztec emperor Moctezuma II, primarily because he believed Cortés was the serpent-god Quetzalcóatl who was prophesied to return that year. The mood changed, however, once Cortés' intentions became clear. By 1521, the Spanish had destroyed Tenochtitlán and its population through war, disease, and the support of Indigenous groups that were enemies of the Aztecs, such as the Tlaxcaltecas and Totonacas.

A New City Rises

Atop the ruins, the Spanish built a new settlement that quickly became the seat of power in the area then known as "New Spain." Land was seized from locals by the new Spanish elite and people were often used as enslaved labor, along-side vast numbers of enslaved Africans. By the 18th century, the new city was the size of Tenochtitlán and was flourishing. To organize society, the Spanish

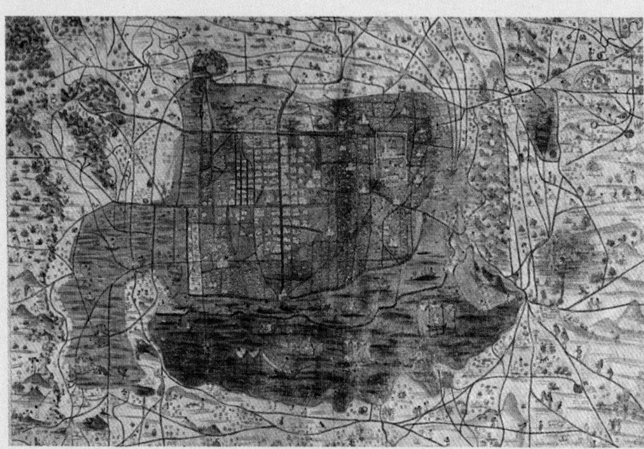

Map showing Mexico City and its surroundings in 1521

Spanish colonizer Hernán Cortés (1488–1547)

implemented a caste system, designed to create complex divisions among the population. As a result, wealth remained in the hands of a few white Europeans and the vast majority of residents lived in squalor. Another, perhaps unforeseen, consequence was the rise of a new creole group, as Spanish-born settlers mixed with locals; this caste was less loyal to the Spanish crown and the white elites.

Independence and Turmoil

By the 19th century, rising taxation, centralized rule from Spain, and a newfound nationalist pride was causing discontent among the creole community. On September 16, 1810, this tension finally erupted into the Mexican War of Independence. After 11 years of fighting, Mexico gained its independence from Spain in 1821, with Mexico City as its capital. However, peace brought with it new problems, and power changed hands 30 times over the next 50 years as politicians and the military jockeyed for control. To compound things, the Mexican–American War saw US troops enter Mexico City in 1847, and the treaty signed after Mexico's defeat forced the government to cede 55 percent of its land to the US. The defeat led to radical reforms under President Benito Juárez, including the separation of church and state, and a reactionary response by conservatives. Their plea for help would

Moments in History

1325
The Aztec capital, Tenochtitlán, is founded on the site of what is now the modern city.

1519–1521
The Spanish conquest under Hernán Cortés destroys the city of Tenochtitlán.

1821
Mexico declares independence from Spain following more than a decade of war.

1848
Defeat in the Mexican–American War results in Mexico losing much of its territory to the US.

1876-1911
Porfirio Díaz established an authoritarian rule during a period known as the Porfiriato, when he served seven terms as president.

1910-1920
The Mexican Revolution lasts a decade but leads to a new constitution and democracy.

1960
Mexico City's popluation reaches 5.5 million, a 1100 percent increase in just 20 years.

1968
Mexico City's Olympics are overshadowed by the Tlatelolco Massacre of students.

1985
An 8.1-magnitude earthquake levels 412 buildings and kills 10,000 people.

2010
Mexico celebrates its bicentennial, with cultural events held across the city.

2024
Claudia Sheinbaum, Mexico City's first female mayor, is elected Mexico's first female president.

result in a French invasion of the city and the four-year rule of Maximilian of Habsburg as Emperor of Mexico.

Porfirio Díaz and Revolution

After years of revolving governments, stability was finally achieved after General Porfirio Díaz appointed himself president in 1876, a position he held for 36 years. During these years, Díaz thoroughly modernized the city and his efforts led to significant advances in the economy, infrastructure, and technology. He was also ruthless, maintaining power by mercilessly dealing with any opposition and keeping wealth in the hands of a few people. Swaths of the population lived in poverty and by 1910 the people had had enough. The resultant Mexican Revolution would force Díaz into exile in 1911, but fighting continued until 1920. In February 1913, war came to the streets of Mexico City during a 10-day battle known as *La Decena Trágica* (The Ten Tragic Days), which destroyed sections of the city and resulted in the overthrow of President Francisco Madero, who had replaced Díaz in 1911. After a decade of intermittent

Devastation from the 1985 earthquake

Celebrating the bicentennial of the 1810 uprising, in the Zocaló

war, peace and democracy were finally established under Álvaro Obregón, a former commander of the revolutionary forces, in 1920.

Fluctuating Fortunes

With war behind it, Mexico City became the center of political and cultural life in Mexico with a growing economy driven by an expanding workforce – the city's population exploded from 500,000 in 1920 to 5.5 million in 1960. It was also a refuge for exiled political thinkers including Leon Trotsky, Fidel and Raúl Castro, and Che Guevara, and the center of a Mexican artistic scene that became world-famous thanks to a generation of dynamic artists that included Frida Kahlo, Diego Rivera, and David Alfaro Siqueiros.

Despite such positives, the city was riddled with corruption, crime, and mass inequality. Repression was rife and in 1968, just 10 days before Mexico City was due to host the Olympics, government forces opened fire on student protesters killing up to 300 people. To make matters worse, the economy was starting to falter and unemployment and inflation were rising. Then in 1985, a huge earthquake leveled large swaths of the city, killing an estimated 10,000 people. Affected areas were quickly rebuilt, but economic difficulties continued despite foreign investment and the 1994 North American Free Trade Agreement.

Mexico City Today

At the start of the 21st century, Mexico City was the largest city in North America, with some 20 million inhabitants. Serious efforts have been made to address the issues of the previous century, and while some solutions have exacerbated inequality, progress is evident. The government has improved the water supply and drainage systems, restored the historic center, improved air quality by pedestrianizing city streets, and reclaimed refinery land for developments such as the Parque Bicentenario. The city has also made progress on social justice issues: same sex marriage was legalized in 2009 and legislation was passed protecting LGBTQ+ rights and decriminalizing abortion. Its first female mayor was elected in 2018, too, Claudia Sheinbaum; she stepped down in 2023 to run as presidential candidate and succeeded, becoming the first woman, and first Jewish, president of Mexico on June 2, 2024.

TOP 10
EXPERIENCES

Planning the perfect trip to Mexico City? Whether you're visiting for the first time or making a return trip, there are some things you simply shouldn't miss out on. To make the most of your time – and to enjoy the very best this city has to offer – be sure to add these experiences to your list.

1 Experience the Zócalo

Mexico City's vast main plaza *(p26)* is the biggest square in the country, and the perfect place to people-watch. Sight-hop around its perimeter, visiting the Palacio Nacional and the Catedral Metropolitana – and make sure you time your visit for the flag ceremony, an impressive display of national pride.

2 Float along the canals of Xochimilco

This ancient canal network *(p42)*, used by the Aztecs, is awash with colorful *trajineras* (skiffs). Pick a "party" boat and drift along to the boisterous beat of a mariachi band, or discover the area's more tranquil side at a local regenerative agricultural project.

3 Tuck into tacos

Mexico City is the taco capital of the world, with a taco stand or *taquería* on every corner and every plaza. These simple corn tortillas *(p74)*, topped with meat or beans, salsa, and a variety of garnishes, are a staple snack – link up with a local guide to find the latest spots, or hunt out your own favorite.

4 Shop at a local market

A centuries-old tradition dating back to the Aztecs, Mexico City's market culture is still going strong. Take a walk through a neighborhood fruit and vegetable market *(p72)*, or take a market and street-food tour, for an introduction to a vibrant slice of daily life in the country's capital.

5 Explore Bosque de Chapultepec

The largest urban park in the Americas *(p36)* could keep you busy for days. Choose from multiple museums, visit the botanical garden, admire mosaics by Diego Rivera, and rent a paddleboat and row round Lago de Chapultepec.

6 Follow in Frida's footsteps

Frida Kahlo was one of the 20th-century's best-known artists, and her works continue to fascinate. Visit Casa Azul *(p34)*, the house she was born (and died) in, and Museo Casa Estudio Diego Rivera y Frida Kahlo *(p109)*, for a closer look at a quite remarkable life.

7 Raise a glass

Mexico is known for tequila and mezcal, but also produces other exceptional spirits such as *sotol*, *bacanora*, *raicilla*, and *pulque*. Let your tastebuds do the testing at one of the city's many rooftop bars – and be sure to say "*¡Salud!*" as you raise your glass.

8 Soak up Mexico City's architecture

From Aztec monuments like Templo Mayor *(p30)* and the colonial-era eye candy of Casa de los Azulejos *(p88)* to architect Luis Barragán's Modernist masterpieces, Mexico City's skyline is studded with extraordinary structures.

9 Tour the top museums

Only Paris has more musuems than Mexico City. You can't hope to visit them all, but seeing the Museo Nacional de Arte *(p87)*, the Museo Nacional de Antropología *(p22)*, and the Museo Universitario Arte Contemporáneo *(p62)* is a fine start.

10 Lose yourself in live music

From traditional mariachi bands to Latin American jazz, classical to hard rock, Mexico City loves its music. Book a table at an intimate jazz club *(p77)*, or grab tickets to a performance at the Palacio de Bellas Artes *(p32)*.

ITINERARIES

Admiring the murals at the Palacio Nacional, feasting on tacos, exploring Condesa: there's a lot to see and do in Mexico City. With places to eat, drink, or shop, these itineraries offer ways to spend 2 days and 4 days in the city.

2 DAYS

Day 1

Morning

The Centro Histórico neighborhood is Mexico City's beating heart. It's the site of the ancient Aztec city of Tenochtitlán and the seat of Mexican government. Start your first day in the Zócalo *(p26)*, timing your visit to this vast central plaza to witness the ultra-formal flag-raising ceremony. Move on to Palacio Nacional *(p26)*, where guided tours take in Diego Rivera's lush, detailed murals celebrating pre-Hispanic and Mexican history and culture. Afterward, head across the street to the Museo SHCP in the Palacio del Arzobispado *(p87)*, where you can enjoy the sculpture of Leonora Carrington and multiple works by Rivera.

Sunrise at the Zocaló's Catedral Metropolitan

EAT
Huitlacoche, corn smut (or corn fungus), is a Mexican delicacy, with an intense nutty flavor. You can try it at Tetetlán *(p119)*, where it's lightly roasted and served with a pineapple puree.

Afternoon

Enjoy lunch at the nearby iconic Café de Tacuba *(p91)*, founded in 1912, followed by a stroll through the galleries of the Museo Nacional de Arte *(p40)*, a gorgeous early 20th-century building whose construction is rivaled only by the artworks hanging on its walls. The restaurant and museum are less than a block apart.

Afterward, take a walk through Casa de los Azulejos *(p88)*, built in 1737. Home to Mexico City's flagship Sanborns general store, the building's exterior is clad in iconic blue-and-white talavera tiles from the state of Puebla. The patio level has an exquisitely designed restaurant, and the bathroom on the mezzanine features a fresco by famed Mexican artist Gabriel Orozco on its exterior.

For dinner, feast on perfectly executed Mexican dishes at Azúl Histórico *(p91)*, located in a colonial-era building that also holds a hotel and hostel, as well as numerous boutiques.

Day 2

Morning

Start your second day with a dawn departure on one of the *trajineras* of Arca Tierra, a regenerative agriculture project in Xochimilco *(p42)*, in the southern part of the city. Guided tours are followed by a meal on the farm. From here, head to the Museo Universitario Arte Contemporáneo *(p62)*, in the Ciudad Universitaria Cultural Center, for the latest in contemporary art. Before leaving the Ciudad Universitaria, check out the stadium mosaic by Diego Rivera.

Afternoon

If you're a serious Rivera fan, consider adding a visit to nearby Parque El Batán *(Av. San Jerónimo 477)*, for another of his fine mosaics. Continue to Jardines de Pedregal to visit the former home of Nobel Prize-winner Gabriel García Márquez, then have dinner at Tetetlán *(p119)*, which is also the site of one of Mexican architect Luis Barragán's iconic structures.

Diners at Tetetlán restaurant, in Jardines del Pedregal

SHOP

Pick up a souvenir or gift of contemporary Mexican textiles, pottery, or woodwork at the Museo Universitario Arte Contemporáneo shop *(muac.unam.mx)*.

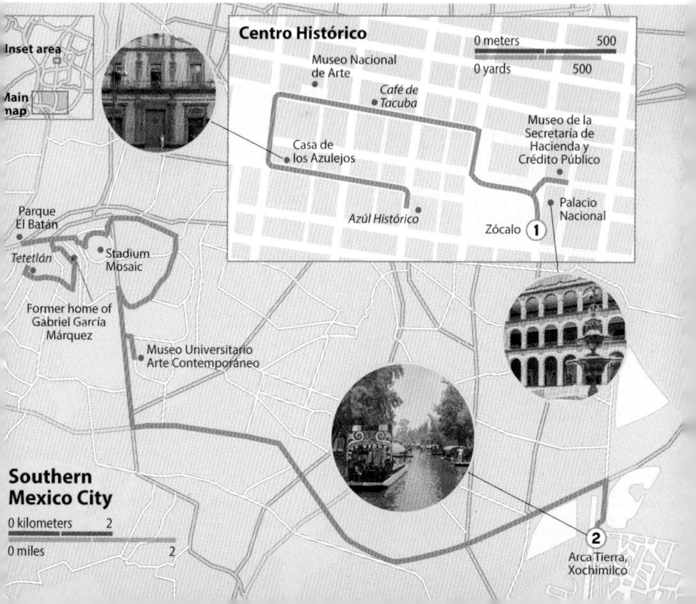

Centro Histórico

0 meters 500
0 yards 500

Museo Nacional de Arte
Café de Tacuba
Casa de los Azulejos
Museo de la Secretaría de Hacienda y Crédito Público
Palacio Nacional
Azúl Histórico
Zócalo 1

Inset area
Main map

Parque El Batán
Tetetlán
Stadium Mosaic
Former home of Gabriel García Márquez
Museo Universitario Arte Contemporáneo
2 Arca Tierra, Xochimilco

Southern Mexico City

0 kilometers 2
0 miles 2

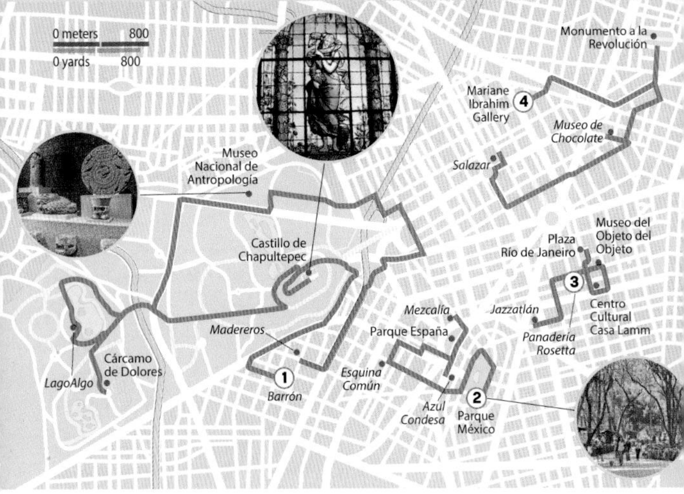

4 DAYS

Museo Nacional de Historia, Castillo de Chapultepec

Day 1

Tuck into breakfast at Barrón *(Calle General Juan Cano 64-Local A)*, next to Bosque de Chapultepec, then take a taxi or car service to Castillo de Chapultepec *(p101)*, which houses the Museo Nacional de Historia. The castle itself is the main attraction, but key objects on display here include the cassock of Fr. José María Morelos y Pavón, who fought for independence. Head west across the park to Cárcamo de Dolores, where you can see murals and a fountain by Diego Rivera. From there, it's a 10-minute walk to lunch at LagoAlgo *(p62)*, overlooking the lake.

A taxi or car service is also the best way to get to the world-class Museo Nacional de Antropología *(p22)*. Be sure to catch a (free) performance of the *voladores de Papantla* while you're there; the ceremony is recognized by UNESCO as a practice of intangible cultural heritage. Finish up with dinner at Madereros *(p119)*, which specializes in wood-fired food.

Day 2

Condesa will be center of attention today. People-watch on Parque México *(p66)* while munching on pastries from neighborhood bakery-cafés Ficelle,

EAT

Nido *(restaurantenido.mx)*, on Parque México, is the restaurant of the culinary school Escuela Superior de Gastronomía. Book the Barra de Maíz, a tasting menu of Mexico's most iconic ingredient: corn.

SHOP
While you're in Juárez, check out FONART and INAH *(p96)*, where arts and crafts and archaeology-themed goods are sold.

Truco, or Odette. Spend time browsing the boutiques on Av. Ámsterdam, a pleasant, shady loop that gives a sense of Condesa's architecture and vibe; the Condesa trolley tour begins and ends right in front of Foro Lindbergh in Parque México. Enjoy lunch on the roof of Esquina Común *(Fernando Montes De Oca 86)*, recently awarded a Michelin star (reserve in advance via socials).

Walk off your meal in pretty Parque España, a 10-minute walk northeast, before enjoying an afternoon mezcal-tasting at Mezcalía *(mezcalia.com)*. From here, it's a short walk to the southern end of the park and your dinner spot: Azul Condesa *(Av Nuevo León 68)*, featuring contemporary Mexican dishes in a classy setting.

Day 3

Begin the day braving the queue at Panadería Rosetta *(Colima 179)*, whose popular baked goods include the *rombo de piña y coco* (pineapple coconut rhombus). From here, it's a two-minute walk to the Museo del Objeto del Objeto *(p94)*, your first art stop of the day, and then just a few minutes more to Centro Cultural Casa Lamm *(casalamm.com.mx)*, where exhibits are housed in a mansion dating to 1911. After lunch at Casa Lamm's restaurant, hop on a bike tour of the Roma neighborhood, which will take you past photogenic sites like the Plaza Río de Janeiro. Finish with dinner and a music set at Jazzatlán *(jazzatlan.club)*, Roma's most intimate jazz club.

Day 4

Start your final day at the Mariane Ibrahim Gallery *(p63)*, whose exhibits include Afro-centric art. A 20-minute walk from here is the Monumento a la Revolución *(p93)*. Buy a ticket that gives you access to the *mirador* (observation deck) and, if you're not afraid of heights, the monument's cupola. Head across Paseo de la Reforma to the Juárez neighborhood for a whirl through the delightful Museo de Chocolate *(p96)*, where you can learn how to make your very own chocolate, before settling down for dinner at Salazar *(salazar.rest)*.

With an extra day, head outside the city to Teotihuacán *(p46)*, a remarkable UNESCO World Heritage Site that's still yielding findings about its past.

Monumento a la Revolución; there are fine views from its cupola

TOP 10 HIGHLIGHTS

Trajineras *(boats) on Xochimilco's canals*

44-109
R TRAVEL
CHIMILCO
ROLIN A
REY
VIVA
LUPI

EXPLORE THE **HIGHLIGHTS**

There are some sights in Mexico City you simply shouldn't miss, and it's these attractions that make the Top 10. Discover what makes each one a must-see on the following pages.

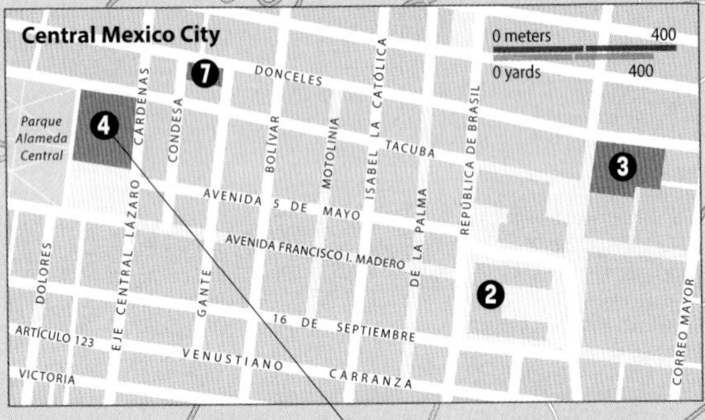

Santa Fe

1. Museo Nacional de Antropología
2. Zócalo
3. Templo Mayor
4. Palacio de Bellas Artes
5. Museo Frida Kahlo
6. Bosque de Chapultepec
7. Museo Nacional de Arte
8. Xochimilco
9. Basílica de Guadalupe
10. Teotihuacán

0 kilometers 2
0 miles 2

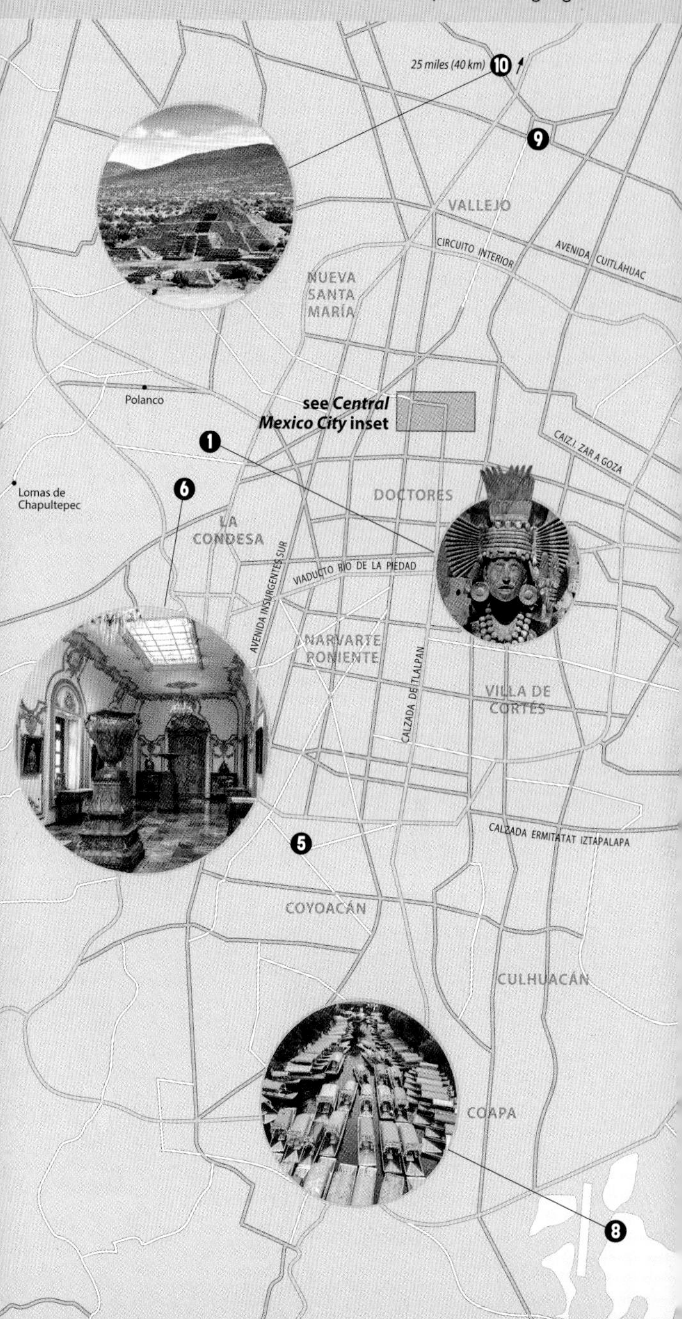
25 miles (40 km) 10
9
VALLEJO
CIRCUITO INTERIOR
AVENIDA CUITLÁHUAC
NUEVA SANTA MARÍA
Polanco
see Central Mexico City inset
1
CALZ. I. ZARAGOZA
6
Lomas de Chapultepec
DOCTORES
LA CONDESA
VIADUCTO RIO DE LA PIEDAD
AVENIDA INSURGENTES SUR
NARVARTE PONIENTE
CALZADA DE TLALPAN
VILLA DE CORTÉS
CALZADA ERMITA IZTAPALAPA
5
COYOACÁN
CULHUACÁN
COAPA
8

MUSEO NACIONAL DE ANTROPOLOGÍA

D3 Av. Paseo de la Reforma & Calzada Gandhi, Chapultepec 9am–6pm Tue–Sun mna.inah.gob.mx

Mexico's ancient civilizations are brought to life through this collection, which is housed in one of the greatest archaeological museums in Mexico. Beneath its hovering canopy, there's an array of priceless treasures, from the huge Aztec Piedra del Sol to a reproduction of Moctezuma's feather headdress.

1 Aztec or Mexica Hall

This is the museum's largest hall, filled with impressive monoliths and finely crafted objects, which represent the diversity of Aztec culture. The centerpiece is the Sun Stone *(p24)*.

EAT

The museum's restaurant, Sala Gastronómica, offers a full lunch buffet as well as salads, sandwiches, and full meals.

2 Oaxaca Hall

Find artifacts from the two cultures that flourished in Oaxaca – Zapotec and Mixtec. There is a reconstruction of the Zapotec Tomb of Monte Albán and many elegant clay vessels. The Mixtec collection has silver and gold pieces, and carved jade and obsidian.

3 Gulf Coast Hall

The Olmecs are known for the colossal stone head sculptures of their leaders, two of which are in this hall.

TOP TIP

Visit the Mexica Hall first to see the fabulous Aztec collection.

Also displayed are stone masks and sculptures.

4 Teotihuacán Hall

The artistic, religious, and architectural objects displayed here reflect the skills of the artisans, and builders of this first great pre-Hispanic city. The monolith of the goddess Chalchiuhtlicue is one of the hall's many highlights.

GALLERY GUIDE

There is a gift shop, temporary exhibition rooms, and a ticket area at the entrance hall, which opens into a huge courtyard. The courtyard's doors lead into the museum halls. Each hall displays archaeological objects from a different region or culture in Mexico. The upper floor is dedicated to the ethnology collection. Outside, within the grounds of the museum, there's a garden area where reconstructions and artifacts are on show.

5 Maya Hall

Examples of ornate temple architecture and artistic creations of Mayan civilization fill the hall. The many stucco figures here illustrate the Mayan ideal of human beauty.

6 Sala Gran Nayar

The Sala Gran Nayar displays objects made and used by four ethnic groups – the Tepehuanes, Mexicaneros, Huichol, and Cora – from the area now known as the state of Nayarit. The fine beadwork of the Huichol is especially interesting.

7 Pueblos Mayas de las Montañas

This exhibit in the museum's ethnology collection features Mayan textiles made in Chiapas, a mountainous state in southern Mexico, as well as pieces from Campeche, Yucatán, Quintana Roo, and Tabasco.

Artifacts from the Temple of Quetzalcóatl

8 El Noroeste: Sierras, Desiertos y Valles

Mountains, deserts, and valleys: these are the landscapes of northwestern Mexico. The crafts from this region differ markedly in material and color compared to other parts of the country. Expect to see woven baskets, instruments, and wooden masks.

9 Pueblos Indios

This hall on the second floor displays *"árboles de vida,"* or "trees of life." These sculpted ceramics visually narrate the creation story, often fusing Catholic and Indigenous beliefs and history.

Tree of Life in Pueblos Indios

10 Los Nahuas

The final hall represents a cultural-linguistic group rather than a geographical region. The Nahua is the largest Indigenous linguistic group in Mexico. The range and variety of items on display include ceramics, woven items, and woodwork.

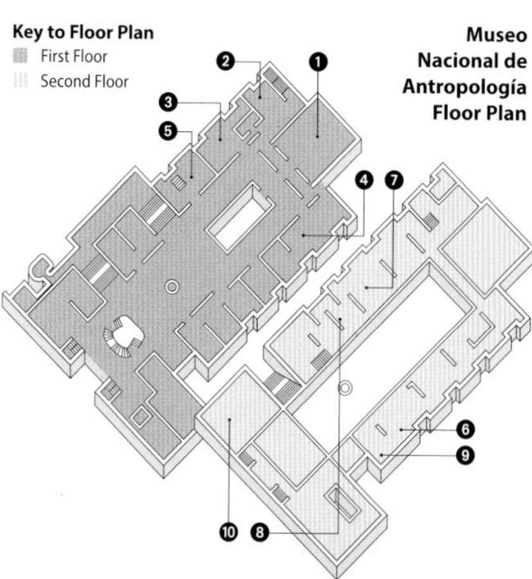

Museo Nacional de Antropología Floor Plan

Aztec or Mexica Hall

1. Sun Stone

This monolith depicts the first four Aztec worlds, said to represent the locations where the Aztecs lived before relocating to Tenochtitlán in 1323. It consists of a central figure, either the sun god or the earth god, surrounded by four squares depicting the four previous worlds. The next set of circles and symbols represent the 365 days of the Aztec year.

2. Coatlicue

Several sculptures of Coatlicue, the mother goddess, who gave birth to the sun, moon, and stars, survive. One sculpture reveals her deadly side, with a head like a snake, a necklace of human hands and hearts, and a skirt of serpents.

3. Tenochtitlán and Tlatelolco

A painting by Luis Covarrubias (1919–87) presents an idealized view of the lake-cities of Tenochtitlán and Tlatelolco before the Spanish conquest. It is based on written descriptions by Cortés and other Spaniards, and offers a glimpse of the lost cities.

4. Obsidian Monkey Vessel

One of the museum's most valuable and most viewed objects, this vessel in the form of a monkey holding its tail in both hands is carved from a single piece of highly polished obsidian. The monkey, in Aztec mythology, is associated with the god of wind and black rain clouds.

5. Headdress of Quetzal Feathers

The headdress on display is a replica of the original that Moctezuma II presented to Cortés. A complete arc of turquoise quetzal feathers is mounted on a headband decorated with red beads, turquoise, and gold.

6. Coyolxauhqui

The huge stone head of Coyolxauhqui, goddess of the moon, depicts her warrior goddess persona. Her cheeks are decorated with rattlesnakes. According to Aztec myth, she was beheaded by her brother, Huitzilopochtli – the sun god – for impeding his birth.

7. Cuauhxicalli of Moctezuma I

Moctezuma I, the fifth Aztec emperor, consolidated the empire. His military victories are displayed on this huge, intricately carved wheel-shaped stone. Eleven historical battle scenes from different parts of Mexico are depicted.

8. Xochipilli

The god of music, song, flowers, and love, Xochipilli sits on his throne decorated with butterflies and flowers, the symbols of his realm.

9. Ocelotl-Cuauhxicalli

A *cuauhxicalli* is a type of altar stone and was used to conduct sacrifices to the gods. The eagle and jaguar are common animal motifs used. Ocelotl was the term used by the Aztecs to refer to all spotted cats, including jaguars.

10. Chapulín

This red-colored stone grasshopper, or *chapulín*, was found on Cerro del Chapulín, Grasshopper Hill, which is the hill in the Bosque de Chapultepec *(p36)*. This place was sacred to the Aztecs and they built a temple here.

Obsidian Monkey Vessel, with mirror polishing

Statue of the goddess Coatlicue

MYTHOLOGY

The Aztecs believed that the world was created by the gods, and that their world was in the fifth and final iteration. The Sun Stone, the monolithic centerpiece of the Aztec Hall, is believed to depict the first four worlds. The heavens were comprised of vertical levels, with the supreme creators, the gods, reigning in the top level. Among the gods, one of the most important was Coatlicue, an Earth goddess who gave birth to the sun, moon, and stars. Another creation myth describes the formation of the world by rival twins, Quetzalcóatl and Tezcatlipoca, representing good and evil. Aztec mythology held that the Universe is comprised of four parts, corresponding to the four cardinal directions, with the convergence ruled from the center by Xiuhtecutli, god of fire and lord of turquoise. The reason that there are often multiple myths explaining single aspects of belief is that the Aztecs borrowed heavily from the Toltec, Teotihuacán, and other cultures. It is estimated that the Aztecs had a pantheon of over 1,500 deities when the Spanish, under the leadership of Hernán Cortés, arrrived in 1519.

Magnificent Sun Stone monolith, Aztec or Mexica Hall

TEMPLO MAYOR

N1 Seminario 8, on the east side of the Catedral Metropolitana 10am–3pm Tue–Sat inah.gob.mx

Although in ruins and surrounded by modern buildings, the remains of the Great Temple still convey the grandeur of the former Aztec city, Tenochtitlán. The museum houses a scale model of the original complex and the giant carved monolith of the goddess Coyolxauhqui.

SITE GUIDE Right at the entrance is the Lacustrine fountain. Turn left and follow the one-way outdoor walkway through the remains; the path ends at the museum's entrance. To visit the eight museum rooms in sequence, turn right at the entrance and watch the video before proceeding up the stairs to room 1. Continue through rooms 2, 3, 4, and 5, then take the stairs back down to rooms 6, 7, and 8.

1 Museo del Templo Mayor

This five-story museum, designed by Mexican architect Pedro Ramírez Vázquez, displays many of the artifacts discovered during the excavation of the temple remains.

2 Monolith of Coyolxauhqui

This magnificent circular carved stone depicts the dismembered Coyolxauhqui, goddess of the moon.

3 Wall of Skulls

During the Aztec times, skulls of sacrificed prisoners were mounted on wooden stakes, forming a *Tzompantli* or a wall of skulls. The museum has a replica of the original wall. In the ruins, there is also a wall of stucco-covered human skulls that forms a side wall of the Tzompantli Altar.

TOP TIP

Visit early morning (or on a cloudy day) to avoid the crowds.

Remains of the Templo Mayor

4 Lacustrine Fountain

Located in the plaza of the site, this fountain has a base that forms a bas-relief map of ancient Tenochtitlán surrounded by the lake, canals, irrigation ditches, and small islands. It gives an overview of the city before the Spanish conquest.

5 Chacmool Carving

This polychrome sculpted figure in a reclining pose cradles a bowl on its belly which was used to hold peaceful offerings to Tláloc.

6 Templo Mayor Construction Stages

The Templo Mayor was enlarged seven times as the stature and prosperity of the Aztecs increased. These enlargements, also known as construction stages, can be seen on a walk through the remains.

7 Tenochtitlán Ceremonial Center

This large-scale model of Templo Mayor creates a visual contrast to the colonial-era buildings in the city. The imposing architecture of the temple and the city of Tenochtitlán were so impressive that the early Spanish colonizers compared it to the great cities of Europe.

Aztec stone carvings in the museum

8 Temple of Tláloc

The Aztecs made peaceful offerings to the Chacmool sculpture in the Temple of Tláloc, god of rain, to ensure successful harvests, fertility, and abundance.

9 Serpent Head Sculptures

Intricately carved and brightly painted stone serpent heads are seen to guard the base of the main staircase of this great Aztec temple.

10 Eagle Knights

Two of these life-size clay sculptures, with five interlocking parts, were found in the House of the Eagles near the temple. One of them is on display in the museum. The Eagle Knights were elite Aztec warriors who dressed as birds of prey.

Clay sculpture of an Eagle Knight

Templo Mayor Floor Plan

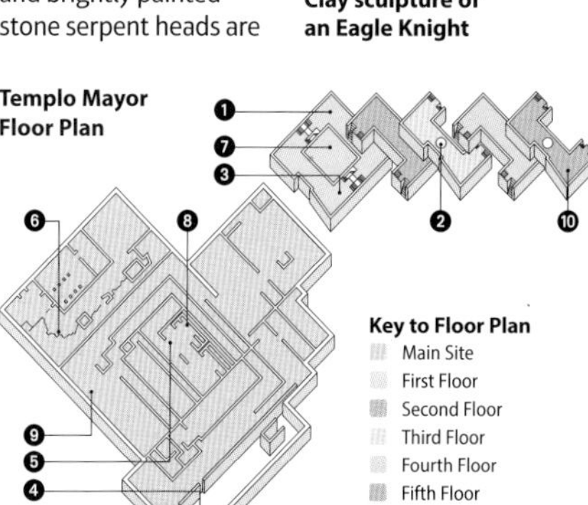

PALACIO DE BELLAS ARTES

L1 · Eje Central Lázaro Cárdenas & Av. Juárez · 10am–6pm Tue–Sun
palacio.inba.gob.mx

This is arguably the most beautiful building in the Centro Histórico. It houses a prestigious collection of Mexican muralist art, and its theater hosts traditional folk dance performances and live classical concerts by world-leading orchestras and artists.

1 Statues of Pegasus

Four sculptures of the winged horse, Pegasus, by Agustín Querol, stand in the esplanade in front of the entrance to the performing arts center.

EAT

Dine in the dazzling Café del Palacio in the lobby, or head to the Café de Bellas Artes for a mid-concert cocktail.

2 Facade Sculptures

The facade has ornate sculptures above the main doorway. In the center, Leonardo Bistolfi's *Birth of Venus* represents harmony. The statues on either side, by Boni, symbolize love and hate.

3 Eagle

On the dome is Geza Marotti's sculpture of the Mexican national symbol, an eagle. It is perched on a cactus, eating a snake. Figures under the eagle represent comedy, tragedy, and lyrical drama.

4 Lobby and Vestibule

A classic Art Deco black marble stairway leads into the vestibule. Across the black-and-white marble floor are the metallic theater doors.

5 Murals

Famous muralists Rufino Tamayo, Diego Rivera, Davíd Alfaro Siqueiros, and José Clemente Orozco painted

Facade of the Palacio de Bellas Artes

huge murals on the walls of the second and third floors. The contrast between the traditional Art Deco interior and the political murals painted with unusually bright colors heightens the dramatic tone in the space.

6 Courtyard

The four-story courtyard is light, airy, and dramatic with red marble columns and a high, four-domed ceiling.

Palacio de Bellas Artes Floor Plan

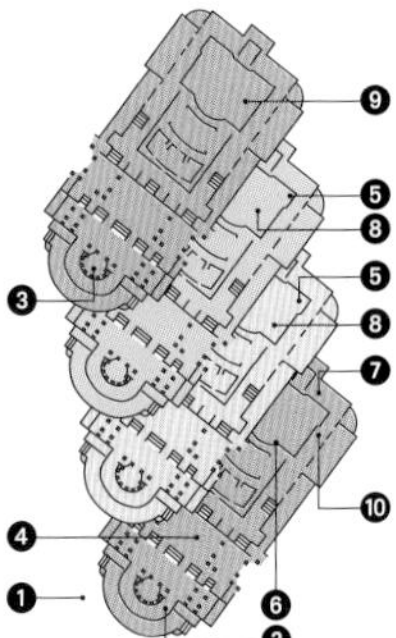

Key to Floor Plan

- First Floor
- Second Floor
- Third Floor
- Fourth Floor

7 Theater

The theater features a crystal ceiling depicting Apollo and the nine muses on Mount Olympus. It also has a stage curtain made by Tiffany & Co. of New York. The depiction of the Valley of Mexico on the curtain is formed with a million pieces of opalescent glass.

8 Art Exhibitions

Several rooms and galleries on the second and third floors host international traveling art exhibitions showcasing masterpieces from all around the world.

9 Museo Nacional de Arquitectura

This museum occupies the fourth floor of the palacio. Changing exhibits feature various aspects of Mexico City, and, occasionally, international architecture.

10 Ballet Folklórico de México

On Wednesday and Sunday evenings, Ballet Folklórico presents folk dances from different regions of Mexico. Colorful costumes, lively music, and stage sets make for fine entertainment.

MURAL CONTROVERSY

Diego Rivera, an avowed communist, was commissioned to paint a mural for the Rockefeller Center, New York. Nelson Rockefeller, a staunch capitalist, approved Rivera's preliminary drawings, but when Rivera later included a portrait of Lenin in the mural, Rockefeller insisted that it be removed. Rivera refused, and the mural was destroyed. A reproduction of it is on the third floor of the palacio with the title *Man, Controller of the Universe*.

Courtyard with marble columns

6

BOSQUE DE CHAPULTEPEC

D4 Main entrance at the west end of Paseo de la Reforma
bosquedechapultepec.mx

The city's biggest park, Chapultepec is a favorite weekend spot for the residents of Mexico City. Its attractions include a boating lake, museums and galleries, and occasionally live, open-air entertainment. The castle terrace offers stunning views across the city.

1 Monumento a Los Niños Héroes

On the eastern entrance to the park *(p103)*, six pillars topped with black eagles commemorate the deaths of six young cadets during the US invasion of Mexico in 1847.

2 Museo de Historia Natural

Several huge pastel-colored domes *(p102)* contain a wealth of exhibits covering the natural world from the creation of the universe to the evolution of life and the world around us.

3 Los Pinos

10am–6pm Tue–Sun lospinos.cultura.gob.mx

This site was the official residence of the president of Mexico from 1934 to 2018. Former president, Andrés Manuel López Obrador (2018–2024) converted this place into a cultural complex and opened it to the public for free. The expansive grounds host fairs and festivals – culinary, cultural, musical – nearly every weekend.

4 Museo Nacional de Antropología

Mexico's largest museum *(p22)*, this archaeological treasure trove has 12 halls filled with artifacts that relate each significant chapter in Mexico's pre-Hispanic human history and ethnography.

Stone sculpture, Museo Nacional de Antropología

Boating at Chapultepec park

5 Lago de Chapultepec, Lago Mayor, and Lago Menor

The lakes are one of the most popular features of the park, and on weekends they take on a festive air. Couples and families walk the shady paths surrounding them or take to the water in colorful rental kayaks, rowboats, and paddleboats. The walkways are filled with vendors.

6 Cencalli: Casa del Maíz

🕒 11am–6pm Tue–Sun

An interactive museum dedicated to Mexico's most important crop – corn. On weekends, the outdoor market features fresh food and locally made handicrafts.

7 Aztlán Parque Urbano

🕒 Noon–8pm Tue–Fri

W aztlanparque urbano.com

Within the Bosque de Chapultepec, this park features a Ferris wheel and other amusement rides and attractions.

8 Fuente de Tláloc

Designed by artist Diego Rivera, this unique tiled fountain *(p103)* in the western part of the park is dedicated to the central Aztec rain god, Tláloc. Several of Rivera's lovely murals can also be seen in the Cárcamo de Dolores, a massive tank behind the fountain.

9 Castillo de Chapultepec

The former residence of Mexican presidents, this stunning castle *(p101)* with manicured gardens now houses the Museo Nacional de Historia.

EAT

If you are hungry, head to LagoAlgo *(p104)* which overlooks the lake. Other options are Del Bosque and Bistro Chapultepec.

10 "Papalote" Museo del Niño

W papalote.org.mx

One of the best children's museums in the city, this colorful and engaging museum has over 250 interactive exhibits based on the themes of science, technology, and art. There is also an IMAX Theater with ten shows daily.

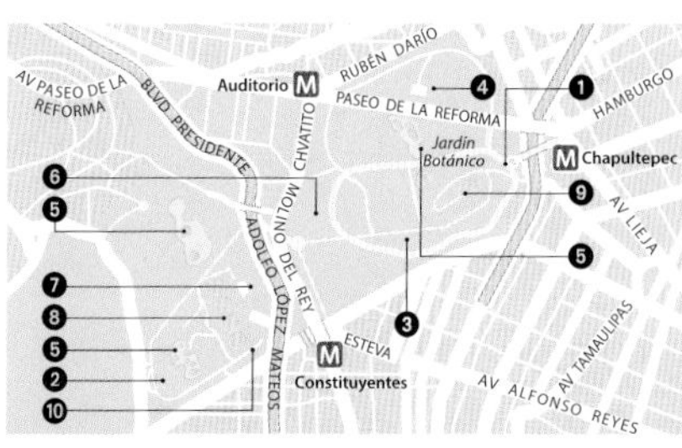

Castillo de Chapultepec

Stained-glass windows in the Castillo de Chapultepec

1. Stained-Glass Windows

The east wing has five exquisite French stained-glass windows. The windows at the top of the Staircase of the Lions have Mexican crests, one of an eagle perched on a cactus devouring a snake, and two with a grasshopper, denoting Chapultepec (Grasshopper) Hill.

2. Casa de los Espejos

This building is also known as the House of Mirrors after the 16 concave and convex mirrors inside. They distort the features of those who look into them.

3. Main Staircase

A double staircase with stone steps and wood-capped brass railings leads to the museum's Castillo Section. The upper level features stained-glass windows.

4. West Terrace

The terrace on the Castillo's west side has a lovely flower garden. The front balcony offers views of Lago de Chapultepec and vistas out across the park.

5. Staircase of the Lions

This staircase with marble lions at the base provides access to the rooftop Garden of the Keep. The staircase was built in 1878 to provide access to the National Observatory. The lions and statuary were added later after renovation.

6. Tall Knight and Garden of the Keep

This formal garden offers views out over the city. The Tall Knight, in the center of the garden, was added in 1876.

7. South Terrace

This terrace houses the Monumento a los Niños Héroes which was added in the 1930s. The Fountain of the Grasshopper is located right in the center.

8. Museo Nacional de Historia – Alcázar Section

The lavish east wing of the Castillo, known as the Alcázar, was once the Presidential Residence and Mansion of Mexican leaders from 1864 through 1939. The personal articles of former Mexican presidents are displayed in 23 opulent rooms.

9. Museo Nacional de Historia – Castillo Section

This section of the museum is based in the oldest portion of the Castillo. The first floor's rooms present Mexico's turbulent history from the Spanish conquest through the Revolution. The second floor has two rooms featuring displays from 1759 to 1917.

10. Museo del Caracol

Located in Section I of the castle, the Galería de Historia is known as the Museo del Caracol because the building is shaped like a snail. A spiral walkway is lined with exhibits that portray the struggle for Mexican independence through the Revolution up to the mid-20th century.

CASTILLO DE CHAPULTEPEC: ALCÁZAR

TOP 10
ALCÁZAR ROOMS

1. Dining Room with china from Díaz era
2. Ambassadors' Reception Hall with French furniture
3. Reading Room with Emperor Maximilian I's monogrammed books
4. Game Room collection gifted to Maximilian I
5. Smoking Room decorated in 19th-century style
6. Carlota's Bedchamber with Maximilian I's magnificent brass bed
7. Council Room and the office used by various former presidents
8. Díaz's Bedchamber decorated in French Empire style
9. Carmen's Bedchamber used by Díaz's wife
10. The President's Office used by Díaz

Caballero Alto tower, Castillo de Chapultepec

Viceroy Bernardo de Gálvez had the first castle built on Chapultepec Hill in 1785, but the building remained unfinished. In 1841 construction resumed, creating a Military Academy. Emperor Maximilian I came into power in 1864 and refurbished the Castillo as his personal residence, creating a luxurious European-style castle with terraced gardens and patios. Expensive furnishings were ordered from Paris, Vienna, and Italy. Later Porfirio Díaz remodeled and extended the castle. The castle continued to be used as a Presidential Mansion until 1939, when President Lázaro Cárdenas moved to a smaller residence and proclaimed the castle as the headquarters of the National History Museum. In 1940 the eastern section, the Alcázar, became a museum illustrating the lifestyle of the former presidents.

Opulent room in the Museo Nacional de Historia

MUSEO NACIONAL DE ARTE

M1 Tacuba 8, Centro 10am–6pm Tue–Sun munal.com.mx

Created in 1982, the National Art Museum is worth a visit for the building alone. The imposing Neo-Classical *palacio* houses the most important Mexican art collection in the world. Encompassing Mexican art from the 16th to the 20th centuries, it features works by the likes of Miguel Cabrera, José María Velasco, and Diego Rivera.

1 Palacio de Comunicaciones

This *palacio*, which houses the museum, is designed in an eclectic style. Its interior features a soaring staircase decorated with intricate wrought iron-work. Glorious paintings adorn the ceilings.

Izaguirre's *The Torture of Cuauhtémoc*

2 The Torture of Cuauhtémoc (1893)

Following the War of Reform in 1861, the new government placed an emphasis on the history of pre-Hispanic Mexico, and by 1893 ancient Mexico was being presented as having had a glorious past. This monumental painting by Leandro Izaguirre depicts the legend of Cuauhtémoc, the last Aztec emperor, and his torture by the Spanish.

MUSEUM GUIDE

Enter the museum from Plaza Manuel Tolsá. Proceed to the grand central staircase, pausing to admire the murals on the ceilings of the reception area and the staircase. The collection includes engravings, cartoons, and folk art, as well as paintings. On the first floor, you will find artworks from the late 18th to mid-20th centuries. The second floor houses art from the late 16th to mid-19th centuries.

3 The Offering (1913)

Saturnino Herrán turned down a scholarship for study in Europe, choosing to remain in Mexico. In this masterpiece of Modernist Nationalism, he captures the unfolding of life. An old man, a youth, and a baby are traveling through life in a Xochimilco-style barge filled with marigolds, flowers traditionally associated with death.

4 The Virgin of the Apocalypse (1760)

Painted at the height of his career, Miguel Cabrera used intense color to portray the theme of *The Virgin of the Apocalypse* triumphing over evil.

5 The Valley of Mexico from the Santa Isabel Mountain Range (1875)

José María Velasco painted this scene to depict the diversity in Mexico's landscape, a first for this skilled artist.

Striking *El Caballito*, Plaza Manuel Tolsá

6 Malgré Tout (1898)

Jesús F. Contreras' Modernist marble sculpture portrays a beautiful woman shackled and bound, still straining and yearning for freedom.

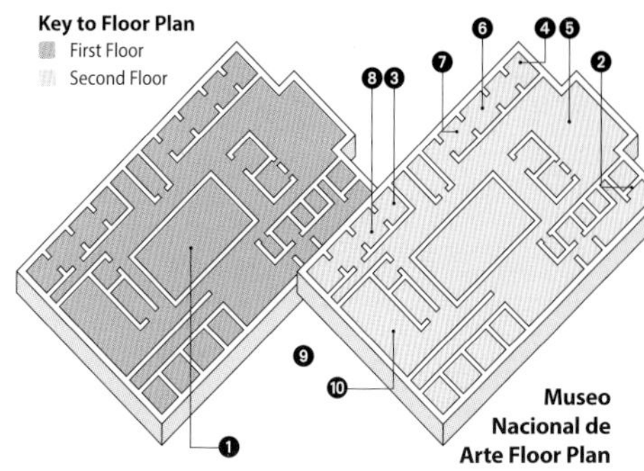

Museo Nacional de Arte Floor Plan

7 Apotheosis of Peace (1903)

In this remarkable work, Alberto Fuster celebrates the years of peace Mexico enjoyed during the reign of Díaz by comparing Mexico to ancient Greece. Neo-Classical in style, the painting mimics the opaque colors found on Renaissance frescoes.

TOP TIP

Check the museum calendar for art workshops, a hit with children.

8 The Cloud (1931)

Gerardo Murillo, best known as Dr. ATL, is one of the most important Mexican landscape artists. He developed Altcolors, a mixture of pigment and resin that he used on a variety of surfaces and especially for his landscapes. *The Cloud* was painted at the height of his prowess.

9 El Caballito (1803)

In front of the museum is the *El Caballito* or "The Little Horse." This statue by Manuel Tolsá shows King Carlos IV of Spain, dressed in Roman clothing astride his horse.

10 The Hot-Air Balloon (1930)

In bright colors and exquisite detail, this painting by Mexican artist Ramón Cano Manilla depicts locals in traditional dress in a rural setting gathering around a hot-air balloon, which is decorated in the national colors.

8

XOCHIMILCO

X4 · 20 miles (30 km) S of Mexico City · xochimilco.df.gob.mx/turismo/index.html

Xochimilco is abuzz with visitors and residents alike, particularly on the weekends. Hop aboard a *trajinera* (flat boat similar to a gondola) to explore Xochimilco's ancient canal network, built during the Aztec empire, and enjoy the floating gardens accompanied by food vendors, flower sellers, and mariachi bands.

1 Boat Rides

A boat trip through the canals in a colorful *trajinera* is the best way to experience the "floating" gardens or *chinampas* (p116) of Xochimilco. The gardens were originally created on a base of aquatic roots that were then covered with soil. Explore the festive commercial area as well as the quieter places farther from the landing.

TOP TIP

In November, local storytellers accompany nighttime boat rides.

2 Embarcaderos and Trajineras

The flat-bottomed *trajineras* are painted with colorful flower motifs. *Embarcaderos* (boat jetties) are found near the center of town – Nativitas is the largest and busiest.

3 Floating Mariachis

Mariachi groups and marimba bands travel up and down the canals. On being hired, the leader boards your boat to dance and sing with the crowd, accompanied by a boatload of musicians tied alongside.

4 Shrines

Small, well-decorated shrines honoring the boaters' patron saints can be found at the *embarcaderos* and along some canals.

5 Floating Food Vendors

Vendors in small boats offer food for your table. Many have kitchens on board with hot soup pots

Rows of *trajineras* on Xochimilco's canals

or grills to serve freshly cooked favorites. Other boats supply beer and soft drinks.

6 Flowers for Women

It is traditional to give flowers to the women in your party, so many flower sellers float past, offering a selection of colorful blooms.

7 Floating Crafts Vendors

Brilliant rugs, colorful ceramics, and all manner of handcrafted items and jewelry are available for sale on small boats. Vendors float by, holding their wares up for all to see, and will come alongside, when invited, to give you a closer look at the selection on offer.

8 Flower Gardens and Nurseries

Lush flower gardens, greenhouses, and nurseries are found all along the banks of the canals. The flowers grown here are shipped across Mexico and throughout the Americas.

> **TRANSPORT**
> The best way to reach and navigate Xochimilco is via taxi or car service *(p122)*. If on a tour, keep a note of the *embarcadero* at the start or finish.

9 Parque Ecológico de Xochimilco

For a different experience, head to this pristine ecological park *(p116)*, popular for bird-watching, for a quiet getaway. The Cuemanco Plant Market nearby is worth a visit, too.

10 Waterside Markets and Restaurants

The *embarcadero* Nativitas has a bustling shoreside market selling souvenirs. There are also restaurants here that can be reached by boat.

Clockwise from right **A mariachi musician; a food stall along one of the canals; charming flower garden; rowing the flat-bottomed *trajinera* on a canal**

BASÍLICA DE SANTA MARÍA DE GUADALUPE

X1 Plaza de las Américas 1 6am–9pm daily virgendeguadalupe.org.mx

This Roman Catholic shrine is a complex of buildings at the foot of Cerro del Tepeyac. In 1531, Juan Diego, an Indigenous man, claimed to have seen a vision of the Holy Virgin, who requested a chapel be built. Over time, pilgrims have come to worship the Virgin of Guadalupe.

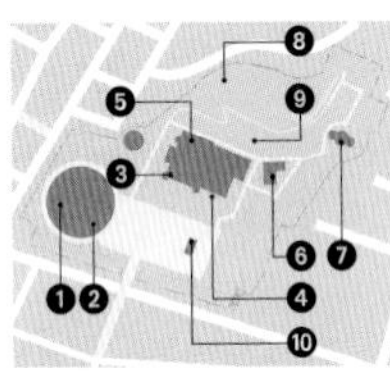

1 Nueva Basílica

This basilica, designed by Mexican architect Pedro Ramírez Vázquez, was consecrated in 1976. The ground here is very soft, and the circular design, symbolizing the universality of God, also helps in evenly distributing the weight of the church.

2 Nuestra Señora de Guadalupe

The original image of the Virgin on the cloak of Juan Diego is mounted high on the wall behind the main altar. Viewers stand on moving walkways that pass below the image.

3 Antigua Basílica

This Baroque temple with four towers and a central tiled dome was consecrated in 1709. Designed by Pedro de Arríeta, the four domed towers and other design elements are similar to those found in the Temple of Solomon in Jerusalem. In 1904 it became a basilica in recognition of the devotion of the faithful. It was reopened in 2000 after being closed for many years, while structural supports were added to protect it from the ever-increasing tilt as it sank into the soft soil.

TOP TIP

Note that in December, thousands of pilgrims visit the basilica *(p79)*.

4 Parroquia de Capuchinas

Initially a convent for Capuchin nuns and then used as a hospital, it became a parish church in 1929.

5 Museo de la Basílica de Guadalupe

The collections in this interesting museum are primarily of artistic religious objects related to Our Lady of Guadalupe. There are paintings, sculptures, textiles, and carvings. There is also a collection of paintings by artists including Cabrera, Villalpando, and Correa.

Worshipers attending mass at the basilica

Striking domes of the basilica

6 Parroquia de Indios

This chapel dates from 1649, and in the small sacristy on the right can be seen the remains of the foundations of the original chapel built in 1531. Juan Diego lived his final years in this place, and the chapel is frequently referred to as the Chapel of Juan Diego.

SHOP

The shop in the Nueva Basílica sells an excellent selection of religious objects, books, and prints related to the Virgin of Guadalupe.

JUAN DIEGO'S VISION

When Juan Diego told the local bishop about his vision of the Virgin, he was met with skepticism. The Virgin reappeared to Diego and told him to gather flowers. Although it was winter, Spanish roses were blooming at Tepeyac. When Diego opened his cloak to show them to the bishop, an image of the Virgin was imprinted on his cloak. He was canonized in 2002, becoming the first Indigenous saint in the Americas.

7 Capilla del Pocito

Our Lady of Guadalupe appeared to Juan Diego at the spring housed in this lovely circular chapel. Built in 1791, the dome is decorated with blue and white tiles.

8 Tepeyac

Juan Diego found the roses which appeared miraculously in winter on the top of the hill of Tepeyac. Capilla del Cerrito was built in 1749 on the site. Fernando Leal painted seven murals depicting the story of the appearance of the Virgin to Juan Diego.

9 Garden and Walkway

A tiled walkway with stairs and ramps was built to direct the flow of people to the Little Hill. Near the base of the staircase leading up the hill is a lovely rose garden. The path returning from the Little Hill curves through a large garden area with fountains and statues.

10 Carrillón

The huge stone cross at the far end of the plaza has bells that ring every hour, and has four different ways of telling the time. There is a modern clock, an astronomical clock, a sun dial, and an Aztec calendar clock with 18 months of 20 days.

TEOTIHUACÁN

X1 Mex 132D (toll), 29 miles (47 km) NE of Mexico City, Mexico State
8am–5pm daily inah.gob.mx

Walking down Teotihuacán's Avenue of the Dead, with one cast pyramid in front and another behind, is one of the most awe-inspiring experiences in the Americas. The magnificent monuments of this ancient site, founded around 150 BCE, bear witness to a fascinating culture that dominated the region for five centuries.

1 Pyramid of the Moon

The oldest and most important pyramid stands at the north end of the Avenue of the Dead. Archaeological excavations have revealed several burial sites within, that have sacrificial victims and exquisite offerings.

2 Pyramid of the Sun

The pyramid's base measures 738 ft (225 m) along each side. A tunnel under the main staircase leads to small chambers of ceremonial importance. A staircase with 248 steep steps and five landings rises 213 ft (65 m) to a flat platform that once supported a temple.

3 Avenue of the Dead

From the Pyramid of the Moon, a 1-mile- (2-km-) long road leads to the Citadel, and continues for another 2 miles (3 km) beyond the excavations. The 131-ft- (40-m-) wide road is lined with nearly identical buildings, which the Aztecs mistakenly believed to be tombs when they named the road. Archaeologists believe that these were

SITE GUIDE

Start at the Temple of Quetzalcóátl. Head north along the Avenue of the Dead, and turn to the right to visit the museum. Next, visit the Pyramid of the Sun. Continue down the Avenue of the Dead to see the Jaguar Mural and Pyramid of the Moon. Finally, explore the structures of the Quetzalpapálotl Palace and complex.

used to house civic, government, and religious functions.

4 Quetzalpapálotl Palace Complex

Three main palaces *(p48)* in the complex are believed to have been the residence of the Pyramid of the Moon's High Priest.

5 Museum

The museum displays artifacts found on-site, along with archaeology, architecture, and history exhibits. The glass floor in the main room covers a scale model of the site. Outside, the shady botanical garden is an excellent place to relax.

6 Temple of Quetzalcoátl

The central pyramid, built in the Ciudadela, around 200 CE, is

Serpent head, Temple of Quetzalcoátl

ornately decorated with sculptures of feathered serpents, the rain god Tláloc, and the mythical crocodile-like symbols for fertile land. Numerous grave sites, containing sacrificial victims and soldiers, have been found within the pyramid.

7 Ciudadela

This huge compound, with its massive central pyramid, is surrounded by walls that measure 1,312 ft (400 m) on each side. These walls were once painted in hematite red and are topped with ornate stone structures.

8 Palace of Temantitla

The most important and colorful murals of the site cover the walls of this dwelling complex. Richly detailed red, green, and yellow murals depict Tláloc and his watery universe. Other murals include a priest sowing seeds and people swimming and playing.

9 Tetitla

Located west of the loop road, this complex of dwellings illustrates how buildings were constructed and reconstructed over hundreds of years. Fragments of intricate murals adorn many of the walls within this compound.

10 Atetelco

This major dwelling complex has its own small altar, and many finely detailed murals depicting jaguars, coyotes, birds, and human figures. The complex is located to the west, across the loop road.

EAT

For lunch, dine at the impressive La Gruta *(lagruta.mx)*, a restaurant located inside a cave on the grounds of the archaeological site.

Monumental Pyramid of the Sun

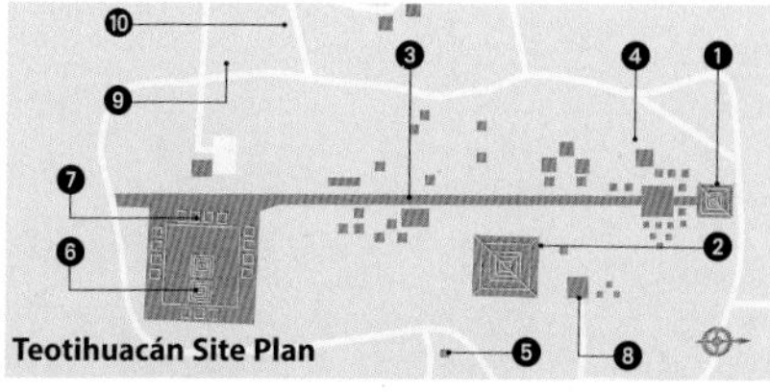

Teotihuacán Site Plan

Intricately carved pillars of the inner portico

Quetzalpapálotl Palace Complex

1. Plaza of the Moon

One of the sacred ceremonial areas in the city, the plaza lies between the Pyramid of the Moon and the Avenue of the Dead. The entrance to the Quetzalpapálotl Palace Complex is reached from the southwest corner of the plaza.

2. Entrance to the Palace of Quetzalpapálotl

A wide stone staircase leads from the Plaza of the Moon up to the covered east portico supported by large columns. The portico opens into a great antechamber that leads into the main palace complex.

3. Stone Serpent's Head

Near the top of the broad stone staircase leading to the portico, a huge carved stone serpent's head emerges from the wall in a position of prominence.

4. Palace of Quetzalpapálotl

The largest and most elegant structure in the palace complex, this is believed to have been the high priest's residence. The original roof burned in the fires that swept through the city in about 750 CE.

5. Patio of the Pillars

The Palace of Quetzalpapálotl is named after the carved bird-butterfly figures that adorn the pillars of the inner portico.

6. Decorative Merlons

The top inner rim of the portico in the Patio of the Pillars features numerous ornately carved stone merlons (battlements) decorated with bas-relief symbols of the calendar.

7. Temple of the Feathered Conches

This temple, located on a level below the palace, features an ornately carved stone facade and pillars decorated with bands of feathered conches and borders of four-petal flower motifs.

8. Mural of Parrot-Like Bird

On the staircase leading to the three-sided courtyard in front of the Temple of the Feathered Conches is a brilliantly colored mural of a parrot-like bird watering a flower with its beak.

9. Jaguar Palace

The palace consists of a large open plaza in front of the middle temple. The nearby staircases have ramps shaped like snakes, while the sloping walls have murals of jaguars in various poses.

10. Jaguar Murals

Murals of jaguars, blowing feathered conch shells and with seashells on their flanks, adorn the sloping walls of a few rooms in the palace. In other murals, jaguars are seen lying in nets in a woman's arms.

HISTORY OF TEOTIHUACÁN

Mystery surrounds the origins of the people who built the city of Teotihuacán. Archaeological finds show that an influx of people from other regions that occurred in 200 BCE resulted in a reorganization of the agricultural groups and development of the new city. The Ceremonial Center has the oldest buildings, with the Pyramid of the Moon being built first, and the Temple of Quetzalcoátl the last. The city was laid out on a grid pattern: the Avenue of the Dead runs north–south, and an east–west road bisects the city. All of the buildings were constructed in the Talud-Tablero style, with sophisticated drainage and sewage systems. Religion was important, and some of the gods honored were Tláloc, god of rain, Chalchiuhtlicue, goddess of water, and Quetzalcoátl, the feathered serpent. Home to skilled artisans and tradesmen, Teotihuacán developed trade throughout Mesoamerica, as its government also extended their rule over neighboring areas. Drought, overpopulation, disease, and social unrest have all been suggested as causes of the city's decline, which started about 650 CE. An extensive fire around 750 CE engulfed much of the city. The buildings were never rebuilt and gradually the city was abandoned.

Awe-inspiring Pyramid of the Sun

TOP 10
STAGES OF DEVELOPMENT

1. 200–150 BCE: Small scattered agricultural settlements.
2. 150–0 BCE: Construction of the Ceremonial Center, Sun Pyramid, and Moon Pyramid begins.
3. 0–150 CE: Completion of Sun and Moon pyramids.
4. 150–200 CE: Planned city developed on a geometric grid; new buildings attached to Sun and Moon pyramids.
5. 200–450 CE: Consolidation of state; government establishes control over economic, political, and religious systems.
6. 450–650 CE: Flourishing economy, expansion of buildings, murals painted, and external expansion of the state.
7. 650–750 CE: Population growth and limited agricultural land pose serious internal crises; colonization and demand for tribute emerge as external threats.
8. 750–800 CE: Decline of the power structure and migration of the officials; the city is damaged by a huge fire.
9. 800–950 CE: Population greatly diminished; city is in ruins and mostly abandoned.
10. After 950 CE: Toltec and later Aztec groups hold the ruins as sacred and use them for their own religious ceremonies.

TOP 10 OF EVERYTHING

Celebrating Día de Muertos (Day of the Dead)

HISTORIC SITES

1 Zócalo

Also known as the Plaza de la Constitución *(p26)*, the Zócalo, in the heart of the Centro Histórico, is one of the biggest public squares in the world. Walking through this open space, visitors can get a sense of city history, with the remains of Aztec temples revealed beneath the Spanish architecture.

2 Iglesia y Hospital de Jesús Nazareno

M2 20 de Noviembre 82
9am–6pm Mon–Sat

This church houses the tomb of Hernán Cortés. Behind the church is the place where Moctezuma II confronted Cortés in 1519. To the south is the Hospital de Jesús Nazareno, built on Cortés' command in 1524 to treat Spanish soldiers.

3 Castillo de Chapultepec

In 1841, this castle *(p101)* was repaired and adapted for use as a military academy. A crucial battle was fought here in 1847, when young army cadets died trying to defend the fortress against invading US troops.

4 Parque Alameda Central

A peaceful park *(p86)* with elegant fountains and shady paths, the Alameda takes its name from the *álamos* (poplar trees) planted in the 16th century. The most imposing monument here is the Hemiciclo a Juárez *(p88)*, built in honor of President Benito Juárez.

5 Monumento a la Revolución

This dome-topped monument *(p93)* celebrates the 1910 revolution that put an end to the *Porfiriato* (Porfirio Díaz's reign). The remains of former revolutionary figures, such as Pancho Villa, Francisco I. Madero, and Lázaro Cárdenas, are interred at the base of the columns. An elevator leads to an observation deck, which offers stunning views. There's also an underground museum.

6 Palacio Nacional

Filling the east side of the Zócalo, this imposing building *(p85)* occupies the former site of the palace of Aztec emperor Moctezuma II, and later the home of Hernán Cortés. In 1562 it became the residence of the viceroys and the headquarters for all of Spain's colonial government in Mexico.

7 Paseo de la Reforma

Built in the 1860s by Emperor Maximilian I, this boulevard *(p92)* was first known as the Causeway of the

***Angel of Independence*, Paseo de la Reforma**

Empress, and was renamed after the restoration of the Republic in 1867. The avenue is studded with monumental statues and fountains, including the golden *Angel of Independence (p93)*.

8 Palacio de Bellas Artes

Italian architect Adamo Boari planned this masterpiece *(p32)* of Art Nouveau construction. The white Carrara marble building has a gleaming triple dome in bronze and an Aztec-influenced Art Deco interior resplendent with red marble.

9 Antiguo Colegio de San Ildefonso

This 16th-century building *(p86)*, originally a Jesuit seminary, is an outstanding example of Mexican civil architecture from the colonial era. The building, now a museum, contains murals by Revueltas and Siquieros, among others.

10 Plaza de Santo Domingo

In 1527, the Dominicans built a convent (the first in New Spain) on this square *(p88)*, of which all that remains today is a restored chapel. It also features buildings that date from the 18th century. Under the arcade sit scribes, who, for a small fee, will fill out official documents using old manual typewriters; the remaining few of a centuries-old tradition.

Hemiciclo a Juárez, Parque Alameda Central

TOP 10 PLACES TO SEE PRE-HISPANIC MEXICO

1. Tlatelolco
The most important Aztec market of Mesoamerica *(p115)* also houses the remains of pyramids.

2. Templo Mayor
The largest and most important temple *(p30)* at the center of Tenochtitlán.

3. Tenochtitlán
The Zócalo *(p26)* sits on part of this site today, which was once the Aztec empire's major market area and site of festivities.

4. Pirámide de Cuicuilco
B4 Blvd Adolfo López Mateos 507, Tlalpan 5606-9758 9am–4:40pm daily
A circular pyramid, this is the earliest known city in the Valley of Mexico.

5. Xochimilco
This network of canals and floating gardens *(p42)* was created by the Xochimilcas.

6. La Pirámide de Ehécatl
Q4 Pino Suárez Metro Station
This small circular structure is a shrine dedicated to the deity Ehécatl.

7. Chapultepec
The hill that forms the highest point of the central valley, Chapultepec *(p36)* used to have a Toltec presence.

8. Tenayuca
Pre-Aztec pyramid *(p115)* with two parallel stairways leading to the temples at the top.

9. Santa Cecilia Acatitlán
One of the few remaining intact pyramid temples in Mexico *(p115)*.

10. Teotihuacán
This archaeological site *(p46)* comprises 8 sq miles (20 sq km) of pyramids and temple ruins.

ARCHITECTURE

1 Bolsa Mexicana de Valores (BMV)

H2 Paseo de la Reforma 255
bmv.com.mx

The wedge-shaped tower and dome of the Mexican Stock Exchange are covered with shimmering black and dark blue mirrored glass. Originally planned as a hotel, the structure was given added height – and its angled appearance – by architect Juan José Díaz Infante.

2 La Lavadora

V3 Vasco de Quiroga 3000

Also known as Calakmul, this cube-shaped structure has been described as one of the strangest in all of Mexico. Its circular cut-outs on each face refer to Maya architecture and cosmology.

3 Torre Mayor

F3 Paseo de la Reforma 505
torremayor.com.mx

Once Mexico City's tallest building, the Torre Mayor towers 740 ft (225 m) above the Reforma. Its facade is made with 323,000 sq ft (30,000 sq m) of glass, supported by a traditional granite skyscraper. The design of this 55-story office building uses anti-seismic technology in order to help it withstand an earthquake of up to 8.5 on the Richter scale.

4 El Pantalón

V3 Paseo de los Tamarindos 400A-Piso 6

Once the city's biggest landfill, Santa Fe has now transformed into a swanky neighborhood. It is known for its innovative architecture, including the "Pantalón" building, so named because it looks like a pair of pants. It's formally called Conjunto Arcos Bosques.

5 Lotería Nacional

K1 Paseo de la Reforma 1
To the public loterianacional.gob.mx

Innovative engineering and Art Deco design elements are highlights of this 1936 building designed by José Antonio Cuevas. It is the first building that used elastic flotation for earthquake protection.

6 Universidad Nacional Autónoma de México (UNAM)

W3 Ciudad Universitaria
8am–8:30pm daily
Public hols unam.mx

In the late 1940s, 60 architects were enlisted to design 20 buildings and sports complexes for the new university to the south of Mexico City. The highlight is the Central Library designed by Juan O'Gorman.

7 Palacio Postal

The main branch of the city's post office *(p88)* has been called one of the capital's most ornate and beautiful

Torre Mayor towering over Paseo de la Reforma

The grand lobby of the Palacio Postal

buildings. It's hard to be superlative in a category with so much competition, but it's true when it comes to this building. Admire the structure and the decor, or schedule a free guided tour to learn more and see the post office's inner sanctum.

8 Museo Casa Luis Barragán

C5 General Francisco Ramírez 12, Ampliación Daniel Garza By appt only; hours vary, check website casaluisbarragan.org

This home and studio, designed by architect Luis Barragán in 1947, was designated a UNESCO World Heritage Site in 2004. The simple masonry building features an orthogonal floor plan with walls painted in bold colors. Light and shadow interplay with the colors and angles, creating dramatic patterns.

9 El Dorito

W2 Bosque de Chapultepec

Mexicans have a nickname for everything. This building, formally known as Torre Virreyes, was built in 2014 and is referred to locally as El Dorito, for its triangle-chip shape.

10 Torre Reforma

F3 Paseo de la Reforma 483

Winner of the 2018 International Highrise Award, this LEED Platinum building has also been recognized for its earthquake-resistant building principles.

CHURCHES

1 Antigua Basílica de Guadalupe

This basilica *(p115)* honors the Virgin of Guadalupe, Mexico's patron saint. In 1531 the Virgin appeared to a shepherd, Juan Diego, requesting a church be built there. Diego convinced the local priest by showing him a cloaklike *tilma* bearing the image of the Virgin. Antigua Basílica de Guadalupe was built in 1709. The *tilma* is displayed in the basilica, built in 1976.

2 Catedral Metropolitana

The largest colonial-era cathedral *(p85)* in the Americas dominates the Zócalo in the center of Mexico City. The Spanish Baroque facade, with 18 bells in its twin bell towers, only hints at the splendor inside.

3 Templo de la Enseñanza

Nine fabulous ultra-Baroque altarpieces fill the interior of this small church *(p88)* built in the 1770s. Angels surround the *Virgin of El Pilar* in the exceptional fresco adorning the high-domed ceiling above the golden main altar, featuring statues of saints. The elaborate late-Baroque facade is unusually narrow and tilts backward from uneven settling.

4 Iglesia y Ex-Convento de San Francisco

L2 Madero 7

One of the best Churrigueresque facades in the city adorns the remnants of the High Convent of Our Holy Father St. Francis of Mexico. Once the largest monastery in the city, it was largely destroyed after the Reform Laws were passed in the late 1850s.

5 Iglesia de la Profesa (San Felipe Neri)

The Mudéjar roof above the choir stalls is the only visible remains of the original 1610 Jesuit church. The church *(p88)* was rebuilt in 1720 and is one of the finest examples of Mexican Baroque architecture. It was consecrated as San Felipe Neri after the Jesuits' expulsion in 1767, but the former name remains in use. The Neo-Classical altarpiece was created by Manuel Tolsá.

6 Iglesia de San Francisco Javier

With a limestone facade and single bell tower, this late 17th-century New Spain Baroque church *(p80)* features a golden main altar with fine decorations. Murals by Miguel Cabrera adorn the cross vaults and the chancel.

Baroque facade of the Templo de Santo Domingo

7 Templo de Santo Domingo

M1 República de Brasil and Belisario Domínguez

The first Dominican church in the city was built here in 1530. The current Baroque church was built in 1736 with a marble carving of Santo Domingo de Guzmán above the entrance. A side chapel contains colorful scarves left by those who have experienced a personal miracle.

8 Templo de Regina Coeli

L3 Regina and Bolívar

This Churrigueresque-style church dates from the 17th century. Three of the five altars display paintings by famous 18th-century artists, including Villalpando and Rodríguez Juárez. The main altar is dedicated to Regina Coeli (Queen of Heaven).

9 Parroquia de San Bernardino de Siena

Dedicated to St Bernardine of Siena, who is believed to have interceded with God on behalf of the Indigenous Mexican people, this Xochimilco church *(p115)* is known for its exceptional altarpiece.

10 Ex-Convento e Iglesia del Carmen

Part of the del Carmen Convent, this Carmelite church *(p108)* from the early 1600s features three exterior domes that dominate the roofline. Built in Latin Cross form, the interior walls of this church are partially tiled with frescoes. The 17th-century main altar is its highlight.

Stunning frescoes in the Templo de la Enseñanza

TOP 10 20TH-CENTURY CHURCHES

1. Santuario de San Cayetano
X1 Av. Montevideo 323
This church was designed by Francisco J. Serrano who was also responsible for El Pantalón *(p54)*.

2. La Iglesia Esperanza de María
W4 Calle Alborada 430
The church grounds feature a café, a gift shop, and a bookstore.

3. Iglesia Santa Cruz del Pedregal
W4 Av. de Las Fuentes 580
There is a chapel dedicated to Mexico's Virgin of Guadalupe here.

4. Templo de la Divina Providencia, El Pañuelito
X2 Cienfuegos 1012
The exterior of this church looks like a pinched handkerchief.

5. La Capilla de San José del Altillo
W3 Av. Universidad 1700
The stained glass of this church has been declared a national landmark.

6. Iglesia de San Ignacio de Loyola
B2 Séneca 306
This church is triangle-shaped, with bright stained-glass panels.

7. Parroquia Emperatriz de América
W3 Calle Mercaderes 99
Find exquisite wooden sculptures by artist Francisco Zúñiga here.

8. Parroquia de Nuestra Señora de Guadalupe Reina del Trabajo
W2 Obrero Popular
This church reflects Alberto González Pozo's commitment to urban design.

9. Iglesia de Santa María de los Apóstoles
X4 Coscomate 120
An unusual structure with a roof that looks like an undulating wave.

10. Iglesia del Divino Niño Jesús
Y3 Calle 47 97, Santa Cruz Meyehualco
The exterior of this church resembles a circus tent.

MUSEUMS

Pre-Hispanic artifacts, Museo Nacional de Antropología

1 Museo Nacional de Antropología

The largest museum *(p22)* in the Americas presents a great display of archaeological artifacts. Each of the museum's halls represents one of the country's prominent pre-Hispanic cultures, including Aztec, Toltec, Mayan, and eight others.

2 Museo de Arte Moderno

Mexico's important contributions to 20th-century modern art are displayed here *(p101)*. The artists featured include Diego Rivera, José Clemente Orozco, David Alfaro Siqueiros, Rufino Tamayo, and Frida Kahlo. There are also large sculptures in the garden.

3 Museo del Perfume

Housed in a gorgeous building in the Centro neighborhood, this museum *(p89)* is appropriately located on Mexico City's "Perfume Street," Calle de Tacuba. It chronicles the history of perfume-making via engaging exhibits, featuring cosmetics and jewelry dating from the end of the 19th century.

4 Museo Franz Mayer

This museum *(p86)* features an incredible collection of decorative furnishings from the 16th through the 19th century. Gleaned from around the world by Franz Mayer, the collection contains exquisite examples of furniture, textiles, silver, ceramics, art, and sculpture. Highlights include a 19th-century Mexican silk shawl and an 18th-century earthenware bowl. There's also a beautiful courtyard. The World Press Photo Exhibition is held here every year.

5 Museo de Arte Carrillo Gil

The permanent collection in this museum *(108)* features paintings by early 20th-century Mexican masters, with a large number of oils by José Clemente Orozco and David Alfaro Siqueiros. These works have amazing scope, including portraits, still lifes, and political subjects. Diego Rivera's Cubist-style 1916 painting,

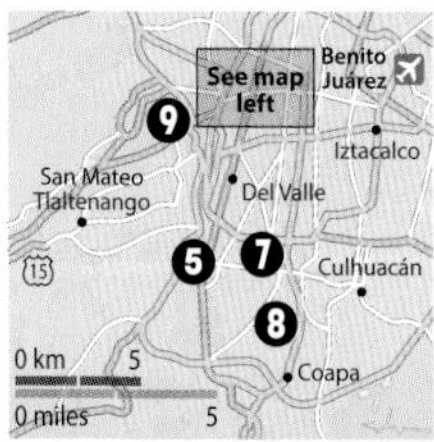

Imposing facade of the Museo Nacional de Historia

El Arquitecto, is displayed here as well. The museum is respected for its exhibitions of contemporary work by international and Mexican artists.

6 Museo Nacional de Arte

This museum *(p40)* showcases the best collection of Mexican art from the past four centuries. Featured are masterpieces by the greatest of the Mexican artists, including the famous muralists, landscape, and religious artists.

7 Museo Frida Kahlo

Paintings by Frida Kahlo and Diego Rivera are displayed in Kahlo's blue house *(p34)*, where she lived and painted. Kahlo's illustrated diary is here, as well as some early sketches, still lifes, and unfinished portraits. Rivera's landscape *La Quebrada* (1956) can also be viewed here.

8 Museo Anahuacallí

Conceived and created by muralist Diego Rivera, this museum *(p107)* was built to house his collection of pre-Hispanic art. Over 2,000 artifacts from the Indigenous civilizations of Mexico, including funerary urns, masks, and sculptures, are displayed across the museum's 23 rooms. The ceiling features exquisite mosaics designed by Rivera in collaboration with architect Juan O'Gorman. There's also a small gallery next to the main building with a changing exhibition dedicated to the Día de los Muertos *(p79)*.

Stone carving, Museo Anahuacallí

9 Museo Nacional de Historia

This museum has two sections – the Alcázar and the Castillo *(p38)*. The vast collections of the museum are housed in the rooms of Castillo de Chapultepec, the former residence of Mexican presidents. The fascinating collections cover four centuries and are arranged chronologically. The Alcázar section is an astonishing house-museum which preserves the lavish lifestyle of Mexico's leaders from 1864 to 1939. The Castillo section offers a glimpse into the turbulent history of Mexico between the Spanish conquest under Cortés and the Mexican Revolution.

10 Museo Rufino Tamayo

A fabulous collection of modern art and sculpture by internationally recognized artists is housed in this dramatic concrete and white marble building *(p101)* set in the woods of the Bosque de Chapultepec. The collection features works by internationally renowned artists Pablo Picasso, Mark Rothko, Joan Miro, Fernando Botero, Isamu Noguchi, and many others. The museum also plays host to world-class traveling art exhibitions several times a year.

Clockwise from above
The Aztec or Mexica Hall gallery in the Museo Nacional de Antropología; a Mayan temple located within the museum's grounds; the large Sun Stone (Aztec calendar), one of the museum's most famous exhibits

ART

1 LagoAlgo

B5 Bosque de Chapultepec, Pista El Sope S/N, Bosque de Chapultepec Section II lago-algo.mx

The iconic building (shaped as a hyperbolic paraboloid) in which this cultural center is housed was constructed in 1964 *(p104)*. Closed for nearly a decade, it reopened in 2022 as a massive contemporary art space, which also features a restaurant overlooking the waters of Bosque de Chapultepec's Lago Mayor.

2 Museo Universitario Arte Contemporáneo

W3 Av. Insurgentes Sur 3000, Ciudad Universitaria Mon & Tue muac.unam.mx

The national university's contemporary art museum has 14 exhibition galleries, many of them super-sized, allowing ambitious group or solo shows of large works like Cai Guo-Qiang's "Resplandor y soledad" and the 2021 multi-media, multi-artist show, "Maternar," an exploration of maternity and motherhood. The museum also has a restaurant and large bookstore.

3 Tetetlán

Another cultural center-restaurant combo, Tetetlán *(p118)* is a charming spot to while away an entire afternoon, especially if you've also made an appointment to visit the adjoining Casa Pedregal by the architect Luis Barragán's. Recent exhibits include Mexican photographer Santiago Arau, whose work explores Mexico's geography and culture and often features iconic sites, such as the Popocatepétl Volcano.

4 Museo Anahuacallí

Muralist and artist Diego Rivera commissioned this pyramid *(p107)* to house his fine collection of pre-Hispanic art, along with some of his own works. The museum's grounds also host festivals, workshops, and live-music events.

Pre-Hispanic art in Diego Rivera's unique Museo Anahuacallí

5 Maison Diez Company

E5 Gobernador José María Tornel 34, Colonia San Miguel Chapultepec diezcompany.mx

If you've never thought of light fixtures as high art, Maison Diez might just change your mind. The Mexican lighting design company installs an annual show inside a mansion with soaring ceilings, creating an immersive experience where lighting is the star of the show. The venue and theme change annually.

6 Art Week CDMX

zsonamaco.com

Each February, Mexico City's museums, galleries, and pop-up projects put on special art shows and a round-the-clock schedule of events, artist talks, and parties. Visitors looking for a single point of entry into the overwhelming schedule might want to check out ZONA MACO, a contemporary art fair (Latin America's largest) that features dozens of international galleries and artists.

7 Mariane Ibrahim Gallery

H2 Río Pánuco 36, Colonia Renacimiento Mon & Sun marianeibrahim.com/es

This gallery, featuring contemporary art by artists of the African diaspora, opened in 2023 to rave reviews, and is the third space (after studios in Paris and Chicago) where gallerist Mariane Ibrahim has hung her works. The art is just one draw, albeit a big one, in this gorgeous mansion. There is also an on-site bookstore, and a restaurant where attention to detail is evident, from artisanal seasonal mezcal cocktails garnished with edible flowers to the perfectly presented asparagus *aguachile* and tuna tartare.

8 Museo de Arte Popular

Spread across several floors, this sprawling museum *(p89)* helps visitors develop an appreciation for the sheer number and variety of Mexican arts and crafts, as well as their makers. On any given day, you might see woodwork, ceramics, paper and cardboard, or metalwork. Particularly fun times to visit are during the annual piñata exhibit, when artists from around the country submit their work in a competition for generous cash prizes, and the yearly parade of carved figures, or *alebrijes*.

Traditional costumes on display in the Museo de Arte Popular

9 Museo de Arte Moderno

One of the many museums in or along the periphery of the Bosque de Chapultepec, this modern-art museum *(p101)* prides itself on accessibility for all visitors, and has exhibits that feature both Mexican and international artists. Don't miss the large sculpture garden, with its many meandering shaded paths, featuring work by artists such as Mathias Goeritz, María Elena Delgado, and Manuel Félguerez, among many others.

10 Museo Universitario del Chopo

This contemporary art museum *(p118)* is housed inside a building that dates to the early 1900s and was brought to Mexico from Germany after an international fair. Many of its exhibits explore themes of gender and sexuality, marginality, and subcultures, both in Mexico and around the globe.

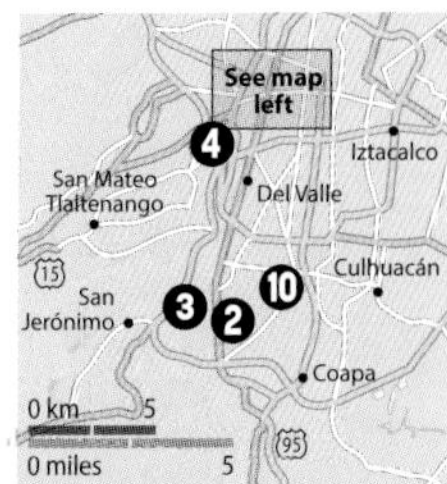

Orozco's mural in the Palacio de Bellas Artes

MURALS

1 Palacio de Bellas Artes

Surrounding the interior courtyard of the *palacio (p32)* are works of seven muralists. David Alfaro Siqueiros' *Nueva Democracia*, Diego Rivera's *El Hombre Contralor del Universo* and José Clemente Orozco's *Mundo Contemporáneo* are the most outstanding

2 Castillo de Chapultepec

On the castle's first floor is the Museo Nacional de Historia *(p38)*, which showcases excellent murals featuring aspects of Mexican history. Juan O'Gorman's *Retablo de la Independencia*, José Clemente Orozco's mural of Benito Juárez, and David Alfaro Siqueiros' satiric image of Porfirio Díaz are a few of the best ones.

3 Polyforum Siqueiros

W3 Av. Insurgentes Sur 701

The interior might be closed to the public while it undergoes renovation, but the eye-catching exterior of this ultra-modern, 12-sided cultural center remains visible. When it is open again, visit to see Siqueiros' masterpiece, the monumental *La Marcha de la Humanidad* or *The March of Humanity*.

4 Antiguo Colegio de San Ildefonso

In 1922, to heal political wounds through art, young artists such as Rivera, Siqueiros, and Orozco were hired to paint murals on the walls of this school *(p86)*. Reaction at the time was mixed, with some disagreeing with the artists' leftist ideals.

5 Casa de los Azulejos

One of José Clemente Orozco's best-known murals, the 1925 *Omniciencia* adorns the staircase of this building *(p88)*, now a Sanborns restaurant *(p91)*. One of his earlier works, it is painted in subdued tones of gold and brown.

6 Museo del Juguete Antiguo México (MUJAM)

L5 Calle Dr Olvera 15, Doctores 5588-2100 9am–5pm Mon–Fri, 9am–4pm Sat, 10am–4pm Sun

The lovely murals painted outside this museum and the surrounding Colonia Doctores neighborhood attract street art lovers from all over. Since 2006, the museum has hosted a street-art initiative, inviting renowned and emerging street artists from around the world to display their work for posterity.

7 Universidad Nacional Autónoma de México

W3 Ciudad Universitaria 8am–9:30pm daily unam.mx

Murals by highly respected artists decorate several university buildings.

On the Rectory Tower is David Alfaro Siqueiros' *Alegoría de la Cultura*. The tiled frescoes on four facades of the Central Library building by Juan O'Gorman depict 400 years of Mexican history. Francisco Eppens Helguera's mural on the facade of the Medicine building portrays pre-Hispanic themes. On the Olympic Stadium is a high relief mural about family, peace, and sports by Diego Rivera.

8 Palacio Nacional

Encompassing three murals and spanning the walls of the central staircase of the Palacio Nacional *(p85)*, the *Epic of the Mexican People* portrays the history of Mexico. It is among Diego Rivera's finest and most visited works. Additional murals fill the walls of the third-floor hallway. Book an appointment in advance; the murals can be visited by guided tours only.

9 Museo Mural Diego Rivera

Diego Rivera's famous *Dream of a Sunday Afternoon in the Alameda Central* was moved here *(p89)* after the earthquake of 1985 destroyed the Hotel Del Prado, where Rivera painted the mural in 1947–8.

10 Museo de Arte Moderno

Oil paintings of many well-known muralists are showcased here *(p101)*, including works by Rivera, Orozco, Siqueiros, Tamayo, and Juan O'Gorman.

TOP 10 MURAL ARTISTS

1. José Clemente Orozco *(1883–1949)*
Best known for his bold murals portraying themes of humanity and industrialization.

2. Diego Rivera *(1886–1957)*
Brilliant muralist and painter, he had Marxist ideals and was a controversial revolutionary.

3. Roberto Montenegro *(1887–1968)*
One of the first muralists, his works dwell on Mexico's traditions.

4. David Alfaro Siqueiros *(1896–1974)*
A political activist, he infused his murals with revolutionary ideas.

5. Manuel Rodríguez Lozano *(1896–1971)*
Dedicated to establishing a true Mexican artistic style, he later protested the monopoly held by the leading muralists.

6. Jean Charlot *(1898–1979)*
French born, he revived and refined the fresco technique later used by Diego Rivera.

7. Rufino Tamayo *(1899–1991)*
Fused Fauvism, Cubism, folk, and pre-Hispanic Mexican styles into his murals and oils.

8. Juan O'Gorman *(1905–82)*
Known for his murals and architecture depicting subjects from Mexican history.

9. González Camarena *(1908–81)*
Indigenous and pre-Hispanic culture were the primary themes in Camarena's vibrant murals.

10. Francisco Eppens Helguera *(1913–90)*
Painter, muralist, and sculptor, his huge outdoor murals are made of colored glass tiles.

Muralist and painter, Diego Rivera

PARKS AND GARDENS

1 Jardín del Centenario

T2 Centenario and Felipe Carillo Puerto

The atrium of the former convent of the church of San Juan Bautista is today a lovely town park in Coyoacán. In the center of the park stands the Fountain of Coyoacán with sculptures of two coyotes.

2 Parque Alameda Central

Landscaped with poplar, ash, willow, and jacaranda trees, this park *(p86)* is a shady oasis adorned with fountains, sculptures, and paved walkways.

3 Parque México

G5 Av. México and Av. Sonora, Condesa

With various activities and plenty of vendors, this park is a lively hub for residents and visitors alike. There are also cafés and shops nearby.

4 Parque Ecológico de Xochimilco

This less-commercialized zone *(p116)* of Xochimilco provides a view of the ancient system of water canals and human-made islands. Pretty flower gardens and a bird preserve are added attractions. Rent a boat or bicycle to explore the canals and walking paths.

5 Parque Lincoln

C3 Emilio Castelar and Luis G. Urbina

Inaugurated by the then-president Lázaro Cárdenas in 1938, this park, in the center of Polanco, is named after the former US president Abraham Lincoln, in honor of his opposition to the US invasion of Mexico in the mid-1800s. It has a small boating lake, a children's playground, and an aviary.

6 Jardín de la Bombilla

Q3 Av. Insurgentes Sur and Arenal

This park has walking paths and benches beneath shady trees. In the center of the park there is a huge monument in memory of Álvaro Obregón, an important figure during the Mexican Revolution, who became president in 1920.

7 Jardín Botánico de Bosque de Chapultepec

D3 9am–6pm Tue–Sun
chapultepec.org.mx/actividad/jardin-botanico

Within the massive Bosque de Chapultepec is the smaller Jardín

Famous floral clock in Parque Hundido

Iconic coyote fountain, Jardín del Centenario

Botánico, which was the country's first botanical garden. It features more than 300 species of plants and trees.

8 Viveros de Coyoacán

S2 8am–5pm daily

Once the private nurseries of environmentalist Miguel Ángel de Quevedo, today this park raises seedling trees for the entire city. Joggers enjoy the mile-long dirt path that curves through the park.

9 Parque Bicentenario

W2 Av. 5 de Mayo 290, Refinería 18 de Marzo, Miguel Hidalgo 7am-6pm Tue-Sun parquebicentenario.com.mx

This 135-acre (55-ha) park, containing seven distinct ecosystems, was built in 2010 to commemorate the country's bicentennial. Built on the grounds of a former petroleum refinery, the park has several conservatories, lots of recreational spaces, and an artificial lake.

10 Parque Hundido

W3 Av. Insurgentes Sur and Av. Porfirio Díaz

A favorite with walkers and joggers, the park was formerly a clay-quarry. More than 50 replicas of pre-Columbian sculptures were placed along the pathways in the 1970s.

TOP 10 COURTYARDS

1. **Plaza de la Santa Veracruz**
L1 Av. Hidalgo
A quiet, pleasant spot to sit and listen to a fountain.

2. **Courtyard of The Shops at Downtown**
M2 Isabel La Católica 30
theshops.mx
Complex in the Centro Histórico with an inviting patio courtyard, and charming boutiques nearby.

3. **Museo Franz Mayer Courtyard**
This museum *(p86)* has a courtyard, which features a tiled stone fountain.

4. **Palacio Nacional**
The inner courtyard of the Palacio Nacional *(p85)* has a fountain and beautiful gardens.

5. **Courtyard of Fonoteca Nacional Mexico's National Audio Archive**
S2 Av. Francisco Sosa 383
fonotecanacional.gob.mx
Spacious courtyard with peaceful walkways.

6. **Sculpture Garden**
K1 Av. Juárez
A garden plaza in Parque Alameda Central with ten huge bronze sculptures.

7. **Courtyard of San Ángel Inn**
Inner courtyard of the former monastery *(p111)*.

8. **Jardín de la Solidaridad**
K1 Zarco y Hidalgo
Commemorates the people who lost their lives in the devastating 1985 earthquake.

9. **Courtyard of the Museo SHCP**
This museum's *(p87)* inner courtyard has ancient trees and stone fountains.

10. **Courtyard of Four Seasons Hotel Mexico City**
Beautiful courtyard with neatly trimmed hedges lining paths that lead to a sparkling fountain *(p131)*.

SPORTS AND OUTDOOR ACTIVITIES

1 Biking

There are many mountain-bike trails near Mexico City. Some of the most accessible are at San Nicolás Totolapan. It offers about 93 miles (150 km) of dirt trails at altitudes between 8,900 ft (2,700 m) and 12,000 ft (3,740 m).

2 Bird-Watching

Mexico City's human population density is high, but so is its fauna, and bird-watchers won't be disappointed. Bosque de Chapultepec *(p36)* hosts bird watching walks, where you might spot one of more than 200 species that call the park home. There are early morning bird-watching tours of Xochimilco's canals *(p42)*, some of which are offered by kayak.

3 Hot-Air Balloons

W flyvolare.com.mx, W volarenglobo.com.mx

If you get your adrenaline rush from floating through the air, a dawn hot-air balloon ride over the Teotihuacán archaeological site *(p46)* is an experience you won't forget. Choose a company with licensed balloon pilots and inquire about what's included in the ticket price – some tours even feature mariachi performances.

Hot-air ballooning over Teotihuacán

4 Rock Climbing

Parque Nacional los Dinamos *(p117)* offers the best (and hardest) rock climbing near the city, with many bolted and bolt-free routes along the narrow gorge of the Magdalena River.

5 Volcano Mountaineering

On a clear day and from a high vantage point, you can see that Mexico City is ringed by mountains, including two volcanoes: Popocatépetl, which is active, and Iztaccíhuatl, which is inactive. Izta-Popo Zoquiapan National Park *(p81)*, two hours from the capital, makes both volcanoes accessible, with plenty of walking and hiking trails.

6 Baseball

W estadioahh.com

While not as popular as soccer, baseball has a major fan base, and Mexico City's Alfredo Harp Helú stadium is the state-of-the-art home to the capital's team, Los Diablos. There are no bad seats, and the fan energy is contagious. On-site concession stands and a club shop round out the offerings here.

7 On Foot

In the city proper, the Bosque de Chapultepec, Viveros de Coyoacán, and the Avenida Ámsterdam loop that rings Parque México are all popular places to walk or jog, and are all well shaded. In the mountains to the southwest of the city limits, the national parks of Desierto de los Leones, los Dinamos, and Cumbres del Ajusco have trails that are suitable for hikers of all levels.

Players from Santos Laguna celebrating a goal in Estadio Azul

8 Soccer

W estadiocdd.com

Whether witnessing a game in a neighborhood park or watching one of the city's big teams, catching a soccer game will be an unforgettable experience. Estadio Azul (also known as Estadio Ciudad de los Deportes) is for professional teams, while Estadio Olímpico Universitario is for college-level teams.

9 Butterfly-Watching

The monarch butterfly migration is one of the most joyful experiences that's easily accessible to Mexico City visitors. While better-known monarch sanctuaries can be found in the state of Michoacán, the neighboring State of Mexico also has several sanctuaries, which make for a perfect day trip.

10 Motorsports

W formula1.com; ahr.mx

F1 is the flagship motorsports event in Mexico City, attracting nearly half a million fans to the Grand Prix each year, which is usually held the last weekend of October. Throughout the rest of the year, the Autódromo Hermanos Rodríguez hosts a number of other motorsports meet-ups, including SpeedFest, which features more than 160 drivers competing in eight categories.

TOP 10 SPORTS STARS

1. Javier Hernández Balcázar
One of Mexico's top soccer players, "Chicharito" plies his trade at Club Deportivo Guadalajara.

2. Sergio "Checo" Pérez
The only Mexican driver on the F1 tour, "Checo" currently races for Red Bull.

3. Braulio Torres-Pérez
Left-handed softball pitcher, lauded for his clean throws, Torres-Pérez has helped Mexico become the 2nd highest ranked team in the world.

4. Citlali Moscote
Long-distance runner Moscote took home the gold medal at the 2023 Pan American Games.

5. Enedina Canul
Canul is one of the protagonists of *Las Amazonas de Yaxunah*, a 2024 documentary that explores women's softball in the Yucatán – and the resistance faced by Canul and her fellow players.

6. Alejandra Orozco
Diver Orozco was due to be one of Mexico's two flag bearers at the 2024 Olympic Games.

7. Santo
Charismatic Santo, who passed away in 1984, was named by ESPN as the "ultimate idol" of *lucha libre*.

8. Renata Zarazúa
Ranked among the world's top 100 women tennis players, Zarazúa represented Mexico at the Olympic Games in 2021.

9. Ignacio Treviño Fuerte
Treviño was due to continue Mexico's long tradition of equestrian sports by competing in the 2024 Paralympics.

10. Santos Saúl Álvarez Barragán
Known as "Canelo," Álvarez is the first – and so far only – boxer to be world undisputed super middleweight champion.

Climbing up Iztaccíhuatl volcano, with Popocatépetl volcano in the distance

MARKETS

1 Jardín de Arte
P3 San Ángel, Plaza del Carmen, bordered by Frontera and Amargura 9am–7pm Sat
This outdoor art market in Plaza del Carmen has artists lining the walkways with their works. The subjects of the paintings range from historical Mexican scenes to contemporary themes.

2 Mercado Jamaica
X3 Guillermo Prieto 45, Jamaica, Venustiano Carranza 8am–4pm daily
Every type of seasonal flower grown in the country can be found at Mercado Jamaica, the city's wholesale flower market. Always excessive, the profusion of blooms of every hue reaches amazing crescendos at major holidays and festivals.

3 Mercado Sonora
X2 South of Mercado de la Merced, across Fray Servando Teresa de Mier 6am–6pm daily
Known as the "Witches Market," locals come to this market to buy a broad variety of herbs, folk medicine, and treatments. Everything required to conjure up love, restore health, or obtain wealth can be found here. – including, controversially, live animals

4 Mercado de Coyoacán
U2 Coyoacán, between Xicoténcatl, Abasolo, Malintzin, and Allende 10am–6pm daily
This attractive neighborhood market offers many traditional Mexican wares, such as sombreros, brilliant rugs, and whimsical piñatas (papier-mâché figures), which can be filled with treats of your liking. The food stalls are a must-visit. There's also a daily craft market at the Jardín del Centenario *(p66)*.

5 Mercado el 100
H5 Calle Orizaba s/n, C. U. Benito Juárez 9am–2pm Sun
W mercadoel100.org
Held every Sunday near the Jardín Ramón López Velarde park, this outdoor farmers' market is so named as all of its merchants sell produce grown within 100 miles (160 km) of the city limits.

6 Mercado Insurgentes
This indoor market *(p96)* is renowned for its glittering displays of fine silver jewelry, pendants, earrings, and bracelets, which are artistically arranged and brightly illuminated. There are also silver bowls, platters, tableware, and sculptures. In some booths you can watch silversmiths at work.

Paintings on sale at the Jardín de Arte

7 Mercado San Juan

An artisans' cooperative, the indoor booths of this market *(p86)* fill two floors, offering traditional handmade goods such as finely crafted silver jewelry, painted ceramics, and handwoven textiles.

8 Mercado de Artesanías de la Ciudadela

Find numerous souvenir and handicraft vendors selling a wide range of traditional items, such as textiles, crafts, and artwork, at this semi-open market in the Centro Histórico area.

9 El Bazaar Sábado

This popular weekly artisan and handicrafts market *(p107)* is only open on Saturdays. It also has a charming courtyard and an excellent restaurant *(p111)*. Just outside the bazaar and around Plaza San Jacinto, there's a *tianguis* (street fair market) with various vendors selling crafts and trinkets.

10 Mercado de la Merced

X2 Rosario and Abraham Olvera 6am–6pm daily

A visit to the city's main wholesale and retail market is as much a cultural experience as it is a shopping one. Its narrow paths are crowded with small booths featuring towering piles of brilliantly colored and artfully displayed merchandise of every kind.

Stall selling spices, Mercado de la Merced

TOP 10 THINGS TO BUY

Colorful ceramic *calavera*

1. Ceramics
Mexico produces a wealth of colorful pottery and ceramics, the Talavera style being the most notable.

2. Woven Fabrics
Look for fine shawls from San Luis Potosí, *panchos* from Saltillo and Zacatecas, and *charro* jackets from Zacatecas and Durango.

3. Chocolate
Chocolate from Tabasco, Chiapas, and Oaxaca is especially prized.

4. Sweets
Sweet breads are offered in dazzling arrays. Fried churros (doughnuts), often dipped in hot chocolate, make a great treat.

5. Jewelry
Silver jewelry of the best quality is readily available. A stamp of "925" indicates the highest silver content.

6. Condiments
Condiments such as jarred salsas make great souvenirs.

7. Leather
Decorative leather jackets, belts, boots, and gloves are popular, as are saddles and bridles.

8. Huichol Art
Highly intricate beadwork on figurines, masks, and ceramics is popular.

9. Liquor and Wine
Tequila and *mezcal* are internationally renowned Mexican liquors.

10. Other Crafts
Exquisite embroidery work, *alebrijes* papier-mâché figures, palma hats, and tin lanterns are also available.

LOCAL DISHES

1 Tacos

Corn tortillas are the base for a near endless variety of toppings: pork, chicken, beef, seafood, beans, or vegetables, which are then dressed with salsas and garnishes of your choice, including onions, tomatoes, lettuce, jalapeños, cheese, and *crema* (a sour cream akin to crème fraîche).

2 Tamales

Tamales are a staple of Mexican life. While there are many regional variations, expect a steamed corn-based dough wrapped in a corn husk or banana leaf and stuffed with a meat, vegetable, and/or sauce filling. Street vendors often sell them as a morning dish for workers, pulled hot and steaming from a giant pot.

3 Pozole

One of the many stews in the Mexican repertoire, the filling *pozole* – like most Mexican dishes – has many variations. Broth is typically pork- or chicken-based, and *pozoles* are usually described as white (no salsa added), green (salsa verde added), or red (salsa roja added). The common ingredient among all styles of *pozole*, however, is the use of hominy, a large corn grain treated with alkali.

4 Mole

Mole is a complex sauce used to accompany meat, fish, or vegetables, or to bathe enchiladas, and it varies by region in terms of key ingredients. The most common moles are red, black, yellow, and green, each featuring a long list of spices, chilis, herbs, and other ingredients, such as chocolate.

5 Churros

A sweet bread treat, churros are deep fried in long, looping hoops of dough, which are then cut and rolled in cinnamon and sugar. They may be served with hot chocolate or dulce de leche. Popular *churrería* El Moro, founded in 1935, has more than a dozen branches around the city; all have a window or spot where you can watch the *churrero* make hot, fresh churros, served up just for you.

6 Frutas Enchiladas

Frutas enchiladas, fresh fruit (think mango, coconut, cactus fruit, and more) dusted with chili powder and a generous squeeze of fresh lime, make for a refreshing snack, especially on a hot day. They are sold by vendors from mobile carts, often around parks.

7 Birria

This dish originated in the state of Jalisco, but is popular in Mexico City. The spicy roasted meat (goat and beef are common) is typically served with its juices, but can also be eaten as a taco or as a "*quesabirria*," a tortilla

Tacos, with spicy salsa and tortilla chips

Sugar-dusted churros with chocolate sauce

filled with the meat, heaped with cheese, and then deep fried.

8 Conchas and Breakfast Pastries

Enter any bakery and prepare to be tempted by an array of sweet breakfast pastries, including the *concha*, a sweet, rounded bun with a topping designed to evoke a seashell. Traditional toppings are vanilla or chocolate, but modern twists include matcha.

9 Ice Cream and Paletas

Ice-cream parlors and popsicle stands are everywhere. Popular chain La Michoacana serves water, cream, and yogurt-based popsicles, many of them studded with treats (think Oreos, kiwi-fruit slices, and gummy bears) that make them as fun to look at as to eat. Upscale scoop shops such as Carmela spotlight Mexican ingredients like hibiscus, lime, and chili.

10 Chapulines, Chicatanas, and Escamoles

While there's growing interest globally in insects and their protein-packed health benefits, Mexicans were way ahead of the curve: they've long been eating *chapulines* (grasshoppers), *chicatanas* (ants), and *escamoles* (ant larvae, often referred to as Mexican caviar). *Chapulines* can be bought in local markets and from street vendors (they come roasted plain or with chili). *Chicatanas* are a delicacy, harvested just one day a year, while *escamoles*, which taste slightly of corn niblets, are served in upscale restaurants.

TOP 10 DRINKS

1. Beer
Mexico produces some of the best beers in the world. Well-known brews include Corona, Dos Equis, and Negra Modelo.

2. Tequila
Mexico's national drink is made by distilling the fermented juices of the blue agave. Fiery and potent, it can sell from $4 to $400 a bottle.

3. Pulque
Made from the fermented sap of the maguey, this drink can be traced back to Aztec times.

4. Horchata
This traditional drink, reputed to be a cure for hangovers, is made from almonds, cinnamon, and cane sugar, and is often served with ice.

5. Wine
Mexico produces over 40 varieties of wines, many of them award-winning.

6. Coffee
Mexican coffee is rich, smooth, and full bodied. A favorite is *café con leche*.

7. Atole
A traditional hot drink made from corn starch, cane sugar, cinnamon, and sometimes chocolate.

8. Hot Chocolate
Traditional Mexican hot chocolate is made from dark chocolate, cane sugar, milk or cream, cinnamon, and ground nuts or eggs for body.

9. Fruit Juice and Licuados
Vendors offer chilled juices, freshly squeezed from a variety of fruits. Mixed with milk, honey, and yogurt, you get *licuados*.

10. Aguas Frescas
Fruit blended with chilled water or mineral water.

Mexican zinfandel

NIGHTS OUT

1 Dance Performances

The acclaimed Ballet Folklórico de México presents fabulously choreographed folk dances within the Art Deco opulence of the theater at the Palacio de Bellas Artes *(p32)*. Classical and modern dance and music performances are also held at the Teatro de la Danza in Polanco. In December, there's a Christmas-themed ballet performance at the Castillo de Chapultepec *(p101)*.

2 Classical Music

One of the world's most spectacular classical concert venues, the Sala Nezahualcóyotl features a gorgeous hall, with 360-degree seating. It is located within the UNAM's *(p54)* cultural center and regularly hosts international performers and orchestras and is also home to the university's philharmonic orchestra.

3 Bars and Lounges

Mexico City is filled with posh cocktail clubs and hidden speakeasies, but the humble *cantina* is still a popular hangout. Spots such as Bar la Ópera *(p91)* and Covadonga *(Puebla 121, Roma Nte)* are old-school favorites, serving *botanas* (snacks) alongside liquor.

4 Noche de Museos

W data.cultura.cdmx.gob.mx/nochedemuseos

Most museums in Mexico City stay open late for the Noche de Museos (Museum Night), which takes place on the last Wednesday of every month. Some museums also have guided tours, concerts, workshops, film screenings, performances, and other activities. Check the website in advance to find out what events are on offer; many of them are free.

5 Clubs

Zona Rosa (p95) is known for club crawling, with a spot for every kind of interest. There are dance, karaoke, LGBTQ+-themed clubs, and more. The nearby Roma neighborhood also has popular dance clubs, including Mama Rumba, where crowds dance until sunrise.

6 Mariachi Music

Plaza Garibaldi is the hub of mariachi music, and roving groups of musicians can be hired for one song or an entire set. Another fun place to enjoy mariachi music is from a *trajinera*, floating on the canals of Xochimilco *(p42)*.

A band of mariachi musicians

Wrestler's mask worn during *lucha libre*

7 Lucha Libre

In this enjoyable spectacle, competing *luchadores* (wrestlers) often wear masks and costumes to create superhero-like personalities. Bouts take place several times a week at the two wrestling arenas close to the historic center: Arena Coliseo and Arena Mexico *(cmll.com)*.

8 Cinema

Going to the movies is still a popular (and relatively affordable) form of entertainment in the city. There are a couple of incredible theaters, including the VIP lounges of Cinépolis *(cinepolis.com.mx)* with its reclining chairs; the charming Cine Tonalá *(cinetonala.mx)* art house, which shows lesser-known films; and the beloved Cineteca Nacional *(p108)*, featuring domestic and international titles.

9 Jazz Music

The city has a great jazz scene and there's no shortage of venues where you can enjoy a show by established or emerging performers. Local favorites are Jazzatlán *(jazzatlan.club)*, which hosts sets every night of the week, and atmospheric Zinco *(zincojazz.com)*, housed inside a former bank vault.

10 Family Evenings

Family fun doesn't have to end when the sun sets. Just hanging out at Foro Lindbergh, the esplanade of Parque México, provides plenty of entertainment. You can watch frisbee players, hula hoopers, and skate-boarders here, and maybe even join in on a game of soccer. Afterward, cross the park for a snack of churros and chocolate at El Moro *(p91)*.

TOP 10 MUSIC AND DANCE VENUES

1. Centro Nacional de las Artes
U1 Av. Río Churubusco 79, Tlalpan cenart.gob.mx
This venue hosts a variety of theatrical and dance shows.

2. Auditorio Nacional
C3 Paseo de la Reforma 50, San Miguel Chapultepec auditorio.com.mx
Enjoy performances in a modern auditorium with excellent acoustics.

3. Centro Cultural Telmex
J3 Av. Cuauhtémoc 19, Juárez 5514-1965
Broadway plays in Spanish are staged at this cultural center.

4. Palacio de Bellas Artes
Dance and music performances are staged at this grand venue *(p32)*.

5. Sala Nezahualcóyotl
W3 Insurgentes Sur 3000, CU, UNAM musica.unam.mx
A concert hall with 2,400 seats.

6. Centro Cultural Ollin Yoliztli
W4 Periférico Sur 5141, Isidro Fabela 5606-3901
This cultural center is a part of an active arts complex.

7. Teatro de la Danza
C3 Centro Cultural del Bosque, Polanco danza.inba.gob.mx
Watch a variety of contemporary dance and musical shows here.

8. El Cantoral
S1 Puente Xoco s/n, Puerta A, Xoco elcantoral.com
An exceptional music venue that hosts classical and contemporary acts.

9. Teatro de los Insurgentes
R1 Av. Insurgentes Sur 1587, San José Insurgentes 5611-4253
This theater hosts a range of plays and musicals.

10. El Lunario
C3 Paseo de la Reforma 50, Bosque de Chapultepec
Top international artists perform at El Lunario.

FESTIVALS AND EVENTS

Bomba Estéreo performing during Vive Latino

1 Día de los Reyes Magos
Jan 6

Three Kings' Day, or Epiphany, is a traditional gift-giving day, when families gather to celebrate. In the days leading up to it, children have their photos taken with the Three Kings, send their gift wish list aloft through balloons, and help select the sweet cakes, *rosca de reyes*, which are served on this day.

2 Art Week
Feb

Art lovers from around the world head to Mexico City for a packed schedule of exhibitions and events during art week. Contemporary art galleries (of which there are many) feature the work of both local and international talents.

3 Vive Latino
Mar

This two-day Latin American rock festival attracts top international music acts representing a wide range of genres, from hip-hop to rock, and ska to reggae.

4 Semana Santa
Mar/Apr

The Holy Week from Palm Sunday to Easter Sunday is an important festival in Mexico. It combines Catholic tradition with pre-Hispanic festivities. Over a million people gather at Iztapalapa, south of downtown Mexico City, for the annual Passion Play. Good Friday is a day of plays and processions.

5 Holy Saturday
Apr

On the Saturday between Good Friday and Easter Sunday, holy vigils and solemn masses are held in many churches. Late at night, participants gather outside as effigies of Judas and other evil forces are burned, signifying the triumph of good over evil.

6 Día del Niño
Apr 30

Día del Niño is the day when children are honored in Mexico. Many museums and cultural institutions host special (and, usually, free) activities and events for children and their families.

7 Festival de México
May 4 W festival.org.mx

Two weeks of concerts and cultural events are held in performing arts venues, historic *palacios*, and in the streets, parks, and plazas of the Centro Histórico during March or early April.

Revelers with *calavera* painted faces, Día de Muertos

8 Formula One

Late Oct

International car-racing fans descend upon Mexico City in droves during the last weekend of October, when Formula One drivers compete for pole position in the Mexico City Grand Prix *(p69)*.

9 Día de Muertos

Nov 1 & 2

The Day of the Dead in Mexico is a two-day celebration to honor deceased relatives and ancestors. Families invite the dead to visit by creating elaborate altars decorated with candy skulls, flowers, and the favorite foods of the departed. It is believed that deceased children return on November 1, and the dead adult relatives and ancestors visit on the next day.

10 Día de Nuestra Señora de Guadalupe

Dec

Pilgrims from across the Americas arrive at the Basílica de Santa María de Guadalupe *(p115)* to honor their patron saint and Mexico's beloved Our Lady of Guadalupe. Most people visit on December 12, the Feast Day of the Virgin of Guadalupe, to attend the midnight mass and thank the Virgin. Pilgrims often complete their journey to the basilica on their knees.

TOP 10 WAYS TO CELEBRATE DÍA DE MUERTOS

1. Try a few pan de muerto
Sample different bakeries' variations of the *pan de muerto* (bread of the dead).

2. Visit the Panteón de Dolores
W2 Av. Constituyentes
The city's largest municipal cemetery draws families who build altars for their loved ones.

3. See the Ofrendas at Sheraton María Isabel
G3 marriott.com
Each year, the hotel creates altars in the lobby, commemorating a particular person.

4. Join the Desfile de Día de Muertos
This parade along Reforma *(p92)* features larger-than-life skeletons and whimsical creatures.

5. Participate in the Desfile de Catrinas
March along the Reforma *(p92)*, past the *Angel of Independence* statue, to the Zócalo *(p26)*.

6. Admire the Ofrenda Monumental en el Zócalo
Every year, Mexican states construct altars that honor deceased key figures at the Zócalo *(p26)*.

7. Stroll in Xochimilco's Marigold Fields
Xochimilco *(p42)* is the best place to see fields of marigolds. It is said that this flower guides the spirits of the dead toward their loved ones.

8. Watch La Llorona
This night show recounts the legend of *La Llorona* (The Crying Woman) in Xochimilco *(p42)*.

9. Hop on a Turibus
Guests dressed in costume are invited to ride free of charge at night on this hop-on-hop-off bus *(p124)*.

10. Explore Museo Anahuacallí
This museum *(p107)* builds *ofrendas* honoring Mexican artists.

DAY TRIPS

1 Teotihuacán

Once the greatest city in Mesoamerica, the ancient ruins *(p46)* form one of the world's biggest and most impressive archaeological zones. Visitors can stroll through ancient palaces, and see fabulous ancient murals.

2 Tepotzotlán

27 miles (44 km) N of Mexico City 9am–5:45pm Tue–Sun tepotzotlan.gob.mx

The highlight of this mountain town, with its pretty plaza and cobblestone streets, is the magnificent Iglesia de San Francisco Javier. Next to the church is the Jesuit college, which houses the Museo Nacional del Virreinato and its collection of historical and religious art.

3 Amecameca

39 miles (63 km) SE of Mexico City

Sitting at the foot of the Popocatépetl and Iztaccíhuatl volcanoes, this town is considered to be part of the Ruta de Volcanes, or Volcano Route. Visit during summer, when you can join local co-ops on a guided tour of firefly sanctuaries (reserve in advance), a magical experience and an important part of local conservation efforts.

4 Malinalco

61 miles (98 km) SW of Mexico City inah.gob.mx/zonas/135-zona-arqueologica-malinalco

One of Mexico's "Pueblos Mágicos" or "Magic Towns," visitors head to Malinalco to see archaeological sites, including Cuauhtinchán. While not as large or as impressive as Uxmal or Chichén Itzá, this site is considered one of the most important ones from the Aztec empire.

5 Cuernavaca

56 miles (90 km) S of Mexico City morelostravel.com

Year-round spring-like weather and a convenient location near Mexico City have attracted the wealthy and powerful to this lovely town for centuries. Conquistador Hernán Cortés built his fortress-like residence, Palacio de Cortés, here in 1522. The town center features a cathedral built in the 1520s and nearby there are two lovely plazas. Palacio de Cortés and Jardín Borda were used by Emperor Maximilian I and his wife Carlota as a retreat. Both are open to the public from Tuesday to Sunday.

6 Valle de Bravo

91 miles (147 km) W of Mexico City valledebravo.com.mx

Wild and beautiful, this area attracts nature lovers and extreme sports enthusiasts. It is popular with power boaters, sailors, hikers, mountain bikers, hang gliders, and parasailers. From December to February the Monarch Butterfly Reserve draws many visitors, who come to witness the amazing sight of millions of the brilliant-orange butterflies cloaking the forests.

Swarm of monarch butterflies in the Valle de Bravo

Colorful row houses lining the streets of Puebla

7 Cholula

Av. Morelos y esquina con 6 Sur, Centro San Pedro Cholula

Located just west of Puebla, this city is known for the Iglesia de Nuestra Señora de los Remedios, a 16th-century Catholic church built atop the Tlachihualtepetl pyramid, whose base is one of the largest in the world. Cholula is full of impressive pre-Hispanic structures.

8 Parque Nacional Desierto de los Leones

X1 Camino al Desierto de los Leones Park: 9am–6pm daily; Monastery: 10am–6pm Tue–Sun gob.mx

Mexico's first national park is a mountainside forest of oak and pine, within which lie the remains of a Carmelite monastery. The monastery dates from 1611, and its name, "Desert of the Lions," refers to the biblical Elijah who lived isolated in the wilderness. Flower gardens surround the monastery, which houses a restaurant offering Mexican favorites. Hiking and biking opportunities abound.

9 Parque Nacional Iztaccíhuatl-Popocatépetl

45 miles (72 km) SE of Mexico City (597) 978-3829 7am–9pm daily

The second- and third-highest peaks in Mexico are in a pine-forested wilderness area with excellent hiking and mountain-biking trails. Paseo de Cortés is another popular place for hiking and mountain biking, with excellent views of the volcanoes.

10 Puebla

81 miles (130 km) E of Mexico City puebla.gob.mx

Puebla is famous for its beautiful colonial-era buildings decorated with hand-painted Talavera tiles. Founded in 1531, the city is nestled between the mountains Popocatépetl, La Malinche, and Iztaccíhuatl. It is known for its street food and traditional restaurants, which serve *mole poblano* (a blend of chilis and chocolate) and *chiles en nogada* (stuffed chilis in walnut sauce). Pueblo also has churches, fine museums, and numerous boutiques offering exquisite Mexican handicrafts and pottery.

AREA BY AREA

Museo Soumaya

CENTRO HISTÓRICO

The seat of government and the neighborhood where history is most palpable, the Historic Center lies on what was once the ceremonial heart of Tenochtitlán, the Aztec capital. The area is so named for the many important buildings that stand here, including palaces, churches, and mansions, some of which have been converted into museums. It remains the heart of the city, mostly thanks to the Zócalo, its principal plaza and social gathering spot, not to mention the cool cafés and shops lining the area's narrow streets.

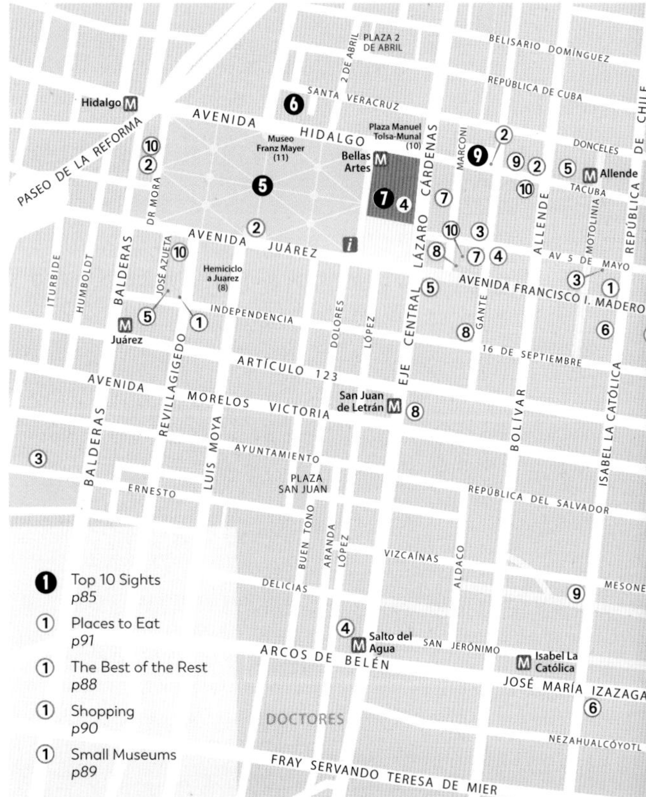

For places to stay in this area, see p130

1 Zócalo

Plaza de la Constitución, also known as Zócalo *(p26)*, was one of the city's main market areas from the days of Tenochtitlán. In the 1860s, Emperor Maximilian I banned merchants and created a Parisian park, with tree-lined walkways and benches. Following the Mexican Revolution the plaza was cleared of all the trees. Today, it is a site for protests and social and political causes.

Ancient Aztec stone statue, Templo Mayor

2 Templo Mayor

This was once the most important temple *(p30)* in the ceremonial complex at the heart of the Aztec empire. In 1978, city workers digging near the Catedral Metropolitana found a carved stone disk over 10 ft (3 m) in diameter, that enabled archaeologists to determine the location of the temple. A major archaeological project ensued, covering several city blocks. Today, visitors can follow a walkway through the excavated ruins and visit a museum that displays the recovered artifacts.

3 Catedral Metropolitana

M2 Zócalo 8am–8pm daily catedralmetropolitana.mx

The largest cathedral in the Western Hemisphere, the Catedral Metropolitana took 240 years to complete. Built on soft, marshy soil, it was sinking until engineers used a variety of techniques to stabilize it. The cathedral still has a visible tilt, but a pendulum hung from the dome marks the slow movement toward the perpendicular. Paintings and religious furnishings adorn the interior.

4 Palacio Nacional

N2 Zócalo Tue–Sun gob.mx/palacionacional

This huge government edifice extends along the length of the Zócalo. Cortés built his palace on the site of the Aztec Emperor Moctezuma II's castle in 1563. The current palace was built in 1693 following fires in 1659 and 1692 which destroyed much of the earlier building. The highlights here are the murals of Diego Rivera, especially his *Epic of the Mexican People (p65)*. Visits are by guided tours only; tickets can be obtained from the Museo de Arte de la SHCP, across the Palacio Nacional – make sure to carry a photo ID.

5 Parque Alameda Central

L1 Av. Júarez, Angela Peralta, Av. Hidalgo, and Dr Mora

The oldest park in the city was established on the site of an Aztec market by the order of Viceroy Don Luis de Velasco in 1590. It was named after the poplar trees planted there. With shade-giving trees and walking paths, the park provides some tranquil respite from the bustle of the city. Fountains and statues adorn the park, including a bronze figure of Neptune, God of the Sea.

ORGAN GRINDERS

As you walk along the bustling streets in Centro you will notice a sound that rises above the various noises of the city. It is the music played by organ grinders hand-cranking old German-made organs. Dressed in beige uniforms they work in teams of two, one turning the crank to produce the music, as the other collects their day's earnings.

6 Museo Franz Mayer

L1 Av. Hidalgo 45 10am–5pm Tue–Fri, 11am–7pm Sat & Sun franzmayer.org.mx

Fabulous decorative arts from the 16th through 19th century are displayed in this former hospital building built in the 18th century. The features of the old building, the archways, carved wooden doors, and frescoes, have been incorporated into the design of the display areas, which tastefully augment the collection of beautiful everyday decorative objects from Mexico, Europe, and Asia.

7 Palacio de Bellas Artes

Built between 1905 and 1934, this stunning performing arts venue *(p32)* presents a fascinating blend of architectural styles. The dazzling Beaux Arts white Italian marble exterior features ornate domes, columns, and European sculptures and carvings. The interior is a superb Art Deco extravaganza, with red marble columns, black marble floors, classic light fixtures, and intricate brass details. Four stories of Art Deco columns, balconies, and grill-work house a spectacular theater, famous murals, fine gift and book shops, and traveling art exhibitions.

8 Antiguo Colegio de San Ildefonso

N1 Justo Sierra 16 10am–7:30pm Tue, 10am–5:30pm Wed–Sun sanildefonso.org.mx

Built as a small Jesuit college in 1588, the building is now best known as the birthplace of the modern muralist movement. Diego Rivera painted his first mural, *The Creation,* here in 1922–3. The walls inside have

works of early muralists such as José Clemente Orozco, David Alfaro Siqueiros, and Fernando Leal.

9 Museo Nacional de Arte

This stunning collection *(p40)* has over 3,000 works by great artists including Miguel Cabrera, José María Velasco, and Diego Rivera. Arranged chronologically, the exhibits focus on the art of New Spain, National Mexican Art, and the modern art that evolved during and after the Revolution. The Neo-Classical building is fabulous, with a double staircase, ornamental ironwork, and beautiful ceiling paintings by Mariano Coppedé (1839–1920).

10 Museo SHCP in the Palacio del Arzobispado

N2 Moneda 4 10:30am–5:30pm Tue–Sun museosdemexico.org

This intriguing museum displays art accepted by the Finance Secretariat in lieu of tax payments. Both famous and little-known artists are on display. Juan Correa's *Nacimiento de la Virgen*, Miguel Cabrera's *Don Juan Antonio*, and Diego Rivera's painting of his San Ángel studio are showcased here. The tax years' collections are kept in a separate gallery.

Art Deco theater at the Palacio de Bellas Artes

AN ALAMEDA CENTRAL STROLL

Morning

Have breakfast in **Casa de los Azulejos** *(p88)*, now a **Sanborns Restaurant** *(p91)*, while admiring the fountain, the intricate tile work, and the mural by Orozco. Across the street is the late Baroque **Iglesia y Ex-Convento de San Francisco** *(p56)* and next door is the **Torre Latinoamericana** *(p88)*. Take the elevator to the 44th floor for a view of the city. Next visit the **Palacio de Bellas Artes** *(p32)* to explore the Beaux Arts building with its Art Deco interior. Catch the murals by Rivera, Siqueiros, Orozco, and Tamayo in the second- and third-floor porticoes. Lunch at the dining room of the *palacio*.

Afternoon

Walk through **Parque Alameda Central**, to the west of the Palacio de Bellas Artes, and enjoy the park's fountains. Next proceed across Avenida Hidalgo to the **Museo Franz Mayer** which houses a great collection of decorative arts. Then head east on Avenida Hidalgo, across Tacuba into the **Palacio Postal** *(p88)*. The Post Office is famous for its stunning staircase and architecture. Then cross Tacuba and walk on to Plaza Manuel Tolsá to the famous statue **El Caballito** or *The Little Horse (p41)* by Manuel Tolsá. Spend the rest of the afternoon at the **Museo Nacional de Arte** *(p40)*.

The Best of the Rest

1. Iglesia de la Profesa

M2 Madero and Isabel la Católica

An early Baroque facade, a Mexican Baroque interior, and a Neo-Classical altarpiece by Manuel Tolsá are highlights of this church.

2. Hemiciclo a Juárez

L1 In Parque Alameda Central on Av. Juárez

This monument was built in honor of President Benito Juárez in 1910. Guillermo de Heredia designed the open semicircle. Italian sculptor Lazzaroni created the sculptures.

3. Plaza Ciudadela and Mercado de Artesanías de la Ciudadela

K2 Balderas s/n and E. Dondé

The largest handicrafts and souvenir market in the downtown area.

4. Mercado San Juan

L2 Ayuntamiento and Aranda

Artisans gather in this indoor market, offering traditional, handcrafted wares.

Dining in the courtyard at Casa de los Azulejos

5. Torre Latinoamericana

L2 Eje Central 2 9am–10pm daily torrelatino.com

Take the elevator to the 44th floor of this slender glass skyscraper for an astounding view of the city.

6. Templo de la Enseñanza

M1 Donceles 104 7:30–8pm Mon–Sat, 10am–2pm Sun

A narrow church with an intricately carved late-Baroque facade, the Templo de la Enseñanza has nine grandiose ultra-Baroque altarpieces.

7. Palacio Postal

L1 Tacuba and Eje Central Lázaro Cárdenas 8am–4pm Mon–Fri, 8am–noon Sat palaciopostal.gob.mx

Completed in 1907, this stunning *palacio*, the main post office, has an amazing central staircase and a luxurious interior.

8. Casa de los Azulejos

L2 Madero 4 7am–11pm

This opulent 18th-century aristocratic residence with a large inner courtyard and exquisitely decorated rooms is sheathed in beautiful decorative blue tiles. It also has a great restaurant *(p91)* on site.

9. Plaza de Santo Domingo

M1

An important site in the colonial era, the Plaza de Santo Domingo is surrounded by austere colonial buildings and the lovely Templo de Santo Domingo in the north.

10. Laboratorio Arte Alameda

K1 Dr Mora 7, Centro 9am–5pm Tue–Sun artealameda.bellasartes.gob.mx

This museum, located in the former convent of San Diego, presents contemporary art through temporary exhibits, screenings, and events.

Small Museums

1. Museo del Perfume
L1 Calle de Tacuba 12, Centro 10am–5pm Tue–Sun museodelperfume.com.mx
Learn more about the art of perfume-making at this museum. It offers workshops where you can blend your own fragrance.

2. Museo Interactivo de Economía
L1 Tacuba 17 9am–6pm Tue–Sun mide.org.mx
The hands-on and easy-to-understand exhibits about economics at this museum are unmissable.

3. Museo Mural Diego Rivera
K1 Balderas y Colón 10am–6pm Tue–Sun inba.gob.mx
This museum houses Diego Rivera's famous mural, *Dream of a Sunday Afternoon in the Alameda Central.*

4. Museo José Luis Cuevas
N2 Academia 13 10am–6pm Tue–Sun museojoseluiscuevas.com.mx
A large collection of works by renowned Mexican artist José Luis Cuevas is displayed here, along with works of other artists.

5. Museo de la Charrería
M3 Isabel la Católica 108 10am–7pm Mon–Fri
The Mexican culture and traditions of the *charrería* (horsemanship) are presented in this museum.

6. Museo de Arte Popular
K2 Revillagigedo 11 (entrance by Independencia) 10am–6pm Tue & Thu–Sun, 10am–9pm Wed map.df.gob.mx
Folk art and handicrafts from across Mexico are showcased in this exceptional museum that is housed in a lovely Art Deco building.

Traditional crafts in the Museo de Arte Popular

7. Casa de la Primera Imprenta
N2 Liceniado Verdad 10 & Moneda 5522-1535 10am–6pm daily Aug
Now a museum, this building housed the first printing press in the Americas.

8. Secretaría de Educación Pública
M1 República de Argentina 28 3003-1000 9am–6pm Mon–Fri
Diego Rivera painted over 100 murals that cover this building's walls.

9. Museo de la Caricatura
M1 Donceles 99, Centro 5704-0459 10am–6pm daily
A fascinating collection of Mexican cartoons is displayed in this museum.

10. Museo de la Ciudad de México y Estudio de Joaquín Clausell
M2 Pino Suárez 30 10am–5:30pm Tue–Sun cultura.df.gob.mx
Find maps, paintings, and early photographs of Mexico City, here.

Traditional baked treats at Dulcería de Celaya

Shopping

1. Plaza de la Belleza
M2 Calle 5 de Febrero No. 40, Centro 10am–8pm daily
This huge shopping arcade is a one-stop shop for a wide range of cosmetics, makeup, and salon services.

2. Perfumeria de Tacuba 13
L1 Calle de Tacuba 13 9am–5pm Mon–Fri tacuba13.com.mx
This old-fashioned perfume shop was founded in 1930. Custom fragrances can be created on the spot here.

3. Dulcería de Celaya
M2 Av. 5 de Mayo 39, Centro dulceriadecelaya.com
Since 1874 this store has specialized in traditional Mexican sweets such as candied nuts and crystallized fruits.

4. Palacio de Bellas Artes Shops
The first floor lobby of this palacio *(p32)* has three shops, an excellent bookstore, a music shop, and a small gift shop.

5. Museo de Arte Popular
Shop for Mexican handicrafts and folk art at this shop located in the lobby of the Museo de Arte Popular *(p89)*.

6. Palacio de Hierro
M2 20 de Noviembre 3 8am–9pm daily elpalaciodehierro.com
Though this upscale department store has branches throughout the city, the Centro store is its flagship and has been in operation since 1891. It offers clothing as well as homeware.

7. Numismática América
L2 Madero 6, Local 6 5510-0790 10am–5:30pm Mon–Fri, 10am–4pm Sat
A haven for coin and currency collectors, this lovely shop's specialty is Mexican currency, though coins from other countries are represented, too.

8. Pastelería Ideal
L2 Av. 16 de Septiembre 18, Centro pasteleriaideal.com.mx
The wedding and birthday cakes sold at this bakery are intricate works of art.

9. Plaza de la Novia
M1 República de Chile 68, Centro 5526-7054 10am–7pm Mon–Sat
Looking for gowns and dresses for special occasions? There's no better place than Plaza de la Novia. Located on "Brides' Street," this mall is named for the sheer number of shops selling wedding dresses and accessories.

10. Sanborns
L2 Calle de Tacuba 2 8am–10pm Sun–Thu, 8am–11pm Fri & Sat sanborns.com.mx
The flagship store of the Sanborns chain offers a wide range of items, including electronics, clothing, books, and toys.

Places to Eat

1. La Casa de las Sirenas

M1 Guatemala 32 lacasadelassirenas.com.mx · $$$

Dine on modern Mexican cuisine, such as cilantro soup and *mole poblano*. There's also a cantina and tequila bar.

2. Los Girasoles

L1 Xicoténcatl 1 losgirasolesmexico.com · $$$

This restaurant offers traditional Mexican cuisine including pre-Hispanic dishes. Salsas, tortilla soup, tamarind mole, and duckling in blackberry sauce are popular.

3. Bar la Ópera

L1 Cinco de Mayo 10 laoperabar.com · $$$

Red booths, polished woodwork, a gleaming long bar, and a bullet hole in the ceiling, courtesy of Pancho Villa, make dining at this historic cantina a luxurious experience.

4. Sanborns in Casa de los Azulejos

L2 Madero 4 · $$

This spot offers traditional Mexican comfort food, as well as international favorites, in an opulent, historical setting.

5. Café de Tacuba

M1 Tacuba 28 cafedetacuba.com.mx · $$

Excellent traditional Mexican entrées like *Oaxacan tamal* and *enchiladas Tacuba* are on offer at a reasonable price.

6. Casino Español

M2 Isabel la Católica 29 1–6pm daily cassatt.mx/restaurante/casino-espa · $$

Enjoy traditional Spanish cuisine with favorites like paella and baked goat.

7. Azul Histórico

M2 Isabel La Católica 30 azul.rest

Situated in the courtyard patio of the Shops at Downtown, this restaurant – one of several run by chef Ricardo Muñoz Zurita – features classical Mexican dishes and great drinks.

PRICE CATEGORIES

For a three-course meal for one, with half a bottle of wine (or equivalent meal), taxes, and extra charges.

$ under $300 **$$** $300–$650
$$$ over $650

8. El Moro

L2 Eje Central Lázaro Cárdenas 42 elmoro.mx · $$

Open since 1935, this place serves churros all through the day. You can watch *churreros* (churro makers) making this beloved late-night snack here. Try the chocolate Mexicano.

9. Coox Hanal

M3 Isabel la Católica 83, 3rd Floor cooxhanal.com · $

Stop by for lunch at this popular place serving Yucatecan specialties such as *cochinita pibil* (slow-roasted pork). Watch out for the fiery salsas!

10. El Cardenal

M1 Palma 23 (between Av. 5 de Mayo & Madero) restauranteelcardenal.com · $$$

Come to this family favorite for such dishes as *flor de maguey* (cactus flower) and *escamoles* (ant eggs).

Enjoying a meal at the historic Café de Tacuba

AROUND PASEO DE LA REFORMA

This is one of Mexico City's most important avenues, which runs through the heart of the city. It's a corridor of big commerce, with soaring skyscrapers packed along its edges, housing international banks and upscale hotels, many of which have earned architectural accolades. On the outskirts are plenty of cool districts with excellent restaurants, bars, and shops, including the LGBTQ+ hotspot Zona Rosa.

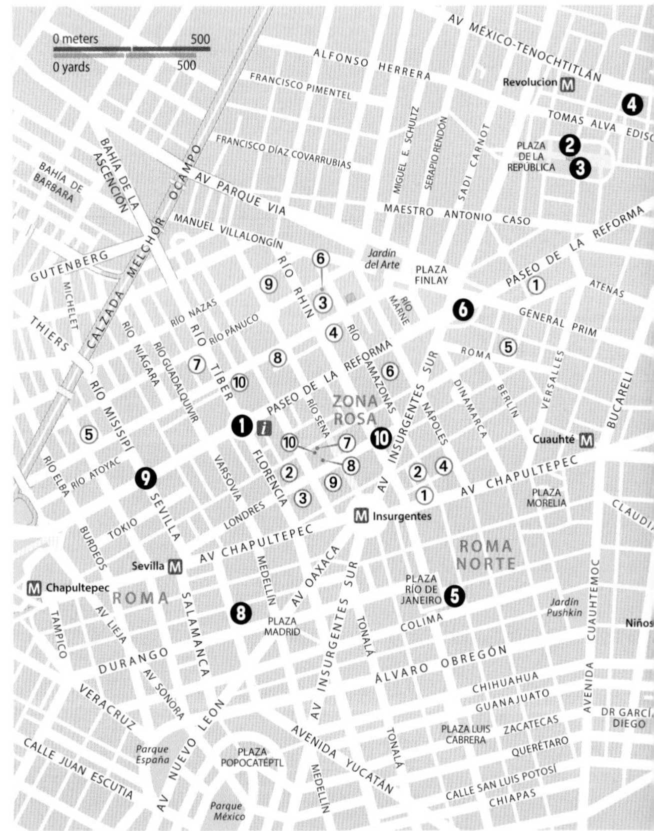

For places to stay in this area, see p131

Monumento a la Independencia, El Ángel

1 Monumento a la Independencia, El Ángel

G3 Paseo de la Reforma, roundabout at Florencia

Known as *El Ángel* for the Winged Victory by artist Enrique Alciati at the top, this monument was inaugurated in 1910 to celebrate Mexico's first century of independence from Spain. The steel column, covered with the names of 24 freedom fighters, is 118 ft (36 m) high.

2 Monumento a la Revolución

J1 Pl. de la República Noon–8pm Mon–Thu, noon–10pm Fri–Sat, 10am–8pm Sun Aug mrm.mx

Built during Porfirio Díaz's reign, this museum was repurposed to memorialize the Revolution and serve as a mausoleum for the remains of the uprising's leaders.

3 Museo Nacional de la Revolución

J1 Plaza de la República, Tabacalera Noon–8pm Mon–Thu, noon–10pm Fri–Sat, 10am–8pm Sun mrm.mx

Set in the basement of the Monumento a la Revolución, this museum chronicles Mexican history from 1867 to the Revolutionary constitution of 1917. The exhibits include photographs, newspaper headlines, historic documents, personal belongings of key figures, guns and rifles used in the battle of 1914, and a reward poster for Pancho Villa dated March 9, 1916.

4 Museo Nacional de San Carlos

J1 Av. Puente de Alvarado 50, Tabacalera 10am–6pm Tue–Sun mnsancarlos.inba.gob.mx

Housed in a Neo-Classical building designed by Manuel Tolsá, this museum houses an impressive collection of European art ranging from the 15th to the early 20th century. Highlights include oils by Rubens, sketches by Goya, and sculptures by Rodin. Entry is free on Sundays.

Fuente de la Diana Cazadora, Paseo de la Reforma

5 Museo del Objeto del Objeto (MODO)

H4 Colima 145, Roma 10am–6pm Tue–Sun elmodo.mx

Mexico's first museum dedicated to artifacts focuses on everyday objects as a reflection of history, culture, and society. It features about 140,000 objects dating to the 19th century. Past exhibitions have included the Mexican presidential campaign "Ephemera," which celebrated objects such as posters, hats, and even cowboy boots. Another exhibition, "Healthy Mind, Healthy Body," presented 3,000 objects related to the history of medicine in Mexico.

6 Monumento a Cuauhtémoc

H2 Paseo de la Reforma, roundabout at Insurgentes Sur

Cuauhtémoc was the last Aztec emperor and led the defense of Tenochtitlán against the Spaniards until he was captured during the final battle at Tlatelolco on August 13, 1521. This monument was designed by Francisco Jiménez and the bronze statue of Cuauhtémoc was sculpted by Miguel Noreña. The bas-reliefs on the base depict the torture of Cuauhtémoc by the Spanish.

Statue of the last Aztec emperor, Cuauhtémoc

7 El Caballito (The Little Horse)

K1 Paseo de la Reforma and Rosales

This bright yellow metallic sculpture by renowned Mexican artist Sebastián was dedicated in 1992. Considered one of his finest works, the statue makes a dramatic statement and dominates the plaza it stands in, with the skyscraper known as the Torre del Caballito behind it. The modern statue represents the head of a horse and replaced a classical sculpture by Manuel Tolsá of Carlos IV on horseback, which had stood there for 127 years, until 1979 when the street was altered. Both sculptures are known as *El Caballito*. Today, Tolsá's original sculpture *(p41)* stands in front of the Museo Nacional de Arte.

8 Casa Museo Guillermo Tovar de Teresa

G4 Valladolid 52-P. B, Roma Norte 10:30am–6:30pm daily

This museum was once the home of Mexican historian and art collector, Guillermo Tovar de Teresa (1956–2013). It features a beautiful library with floor-to-ceiling bookshelves. Tovar's photographs and books make up one of the most important collections in Latin America. There's a lovely courtyard garden, too.

BIKE AROUND PASEO DE LA REFORMA

Morning

Start your day by having breakfast at **Pánuco 36** *(p97)*, which is part of the **Mariane Ibrahim Gallery** *(p63)*. Enjoy the latest art exhibition at the gallery before getting on an Ecobici a few blocks away at the docking station on Río Pánuco between Río Tigris and Río Sena. Next, make your way to **Plaza de la Lectura José Saramago**. Take a turn through this pocket park, dedicated to the Portuguese Nobel Prize novelist. There's also a commemorative plaque and column in memory of the author here.

Afternoon

Ride a bit farther up Reforma and along the edge of the **Bosque de Chapultepec** *(p36)*. Dock your bike at the Ecobici station just beyond the **Museo de Arte Moderno** *(p101)*. You can skip the indoor exhibits and walk through the museum's large sculpture garden. Pick up another bike, and take the bike lane down the Paseo de la Reforma. This pleasant path goes past the **Fuente de la Diana Cazadora** and **Monumento a la Independencia, El Ángel** *(p93)*. Head toward Colonia Juárez, setting your sights on lunch at **Masala y Maíz** *(p97)*. The nearest docking station is at Marsella and Napolés. After lunch, hop on a bike at the same station and head to **Mercado de Artesanías de la Ciudadela** *(p88)*, a popular handicraft market.

9 Fuente de la Diana Cazadora

G3 Paseo de la Reforma, roundabout at Río Rhin

A statue of Roman goddess Diana the Huntress, sculpted by John Olaguíbel, adorns the fountain in the westernmost roundabout. The nude depiction of Diana created debate and controversy in 1942, and finally the artist covered her loins with a bronze covering, which remained in place until 1967. The stone fountain was designed by architect Vicente Mendiola.

10 Zona Rosa

H3 Paseo de la Reforma, Niza, Av. Chapultepec & Varsovia

Once a trendy neighborhood of first-class hotels and restaurants, sidewalk cafés, and boutiques, Zona Rosa, the Pink Zone, is studded with bars and nightclubs and has long been the boisterous hub of LGTBQ+ nightlife in Mexico City.

THE PINK ZONE

Most clubs in the Zona Rosa have loud music, energetic dancing, and packed crowds. There are many to choose from, but local favorites include Cabaretito, featuring drag shows, DJs, and gogo dancers; Kinky, which is spread over three floors; and El Almacén, offering live shows.

Shopping

1. FONART

J2 Paseo de la Reforma 116
gob.mx/fonart

One of the best stores for Mexican handicrafts – everything from ceramics to woven baskets is available here.

2. Plaza del Ángel

G3 Londres 161, Juárez

This plaza houses some 30 antique shops selling a selection of fine antiques, including porcelain, oil paintings, furniture, and silver.

3. Mercado Insurgentes

G3 Londres 160 and Liverpool 161

A fun place to shop for silver jewelry, sculpture, and tableware, this market has some 200 booths.

4. JPEG

H3 Calle Marsella 57, Juárez jpeg.mx

Trendy Mexican streetwear brand JPEG is known for its clothing, jewelry, accessories, and household goods.

5. Museo de Chocolate

J2 Calle Milan 45, Juárez
mucho.org.mx

Small but delicious varieties of Mexican chocolates and other sweet treats can be tried at this engaging museum.

6. Reforma 222

H2 Paseo de la Reforma 222
reforma222.com

A multilevel shopping mall with several fashion brands, a cinema, and international restaurants.

7. INAH Tienda

G3 Hamburgo 135, Juárez
5541-6607

INAH sells a range of archaeology-themed books, field guides, and maps.

8. Plaza la Rosa

H3 Between Amberes and Génova, Juárez

This lively shopping center offers dozens of brand-name clothing stores.

9. Sanborns

J2 Paseo de la Reforma 45
sanborns.com.mx

A one-stop shop, this department store has a restaurant, a pharmacy, a bookstore, and a gift shop.

10. El Péndulo

H3 Hamburgo 126, Juárez
pendulo.com

In addition to a wide range of books, this store has an attractive café. Grab a coffee and get lost in the pages of your purchase.

Antique shop in the Plaza del Ángel

Places to Eat

PRICE CATEGORIES

For a three-course meal for one, with half a bottle of wine (or equivalent meal), taxes, and extra charges.

$ under $300 $$ $300–$650
$$$ over $650

1. Masala y Maíz

H3 Calle Marsella 72, Juárez Tue masalaymaiz.com • $$

Owned by a Mexican and an American-born chef with South Asian and African roots, the menu includes dishes like *pipian* paneer with sweet potato, *verdolagas* (purslane), and curry leaf.

2. Pánuco 36

H2 Río Pánuco 36, Renacimiento 5592-3363 Mon & Sun • $$

Set in the Marine Ibrahim Gallery, this café *(p63)* has an internationally inspired breakfast and a great lunch menu.

3. La Provoleta

H2 Rio Rhin 72, Renacimiento lp.resto.marketing/laprovoletarhin • $$

An Argentinian restaurant specializing in grilled meats served while still sizzling.

4. Havre 77

H3 Havre 77, Juárez Mon havre77.mx • $$$

Housed in a 19th-century mansion, this popular French-inspired restaurant has a menu offering everything from escargots and French onion soup to *sole a la Meuniere* (classic fish dish).

5. Chu-Cho

G3 Calle Río Lerma 144, Cuauhtémoc 5525-6118 • $

This churro shop is known for its creative interpretations and churro add-ons. Heart-shaped churros, dipped in pink-and-white sprinkles for Valentine's Day, and churros filled with dulce de leche are just some of the treats you can enjoy here.

Elegant interior of French-style restaurant Havre 77

6. Le Tachinomi Desu

G2 Río Pánuco 132-1a, Cuauhtémoc Sun edokobayashi.com • $$

This tiny standing bar has an excellent Japanese whiskey and sake selection, as well as an omakase menu.

7. YOOZOO

H2 Río Pánuco 32, Renacimiento yoozoo.mx • $

The flavors at this trendy *boba* tea shop include *horchata*, a Mexican drink made with rice, cinnamon, and sugar.

8. Taquería Gabriel

G2 Calle Río Sena 87-Local A, Cuauhtémoc 5207-6276 • $

There's plenty of great tacos on the menu at Gabriel's, all of which are packed full of flavor.

9. Doña Blanca

G5 Calle Río Lerma 271, Cuauhtémoc fondadonablanca.com • $

Savor traditional Mexican dishes at this breakfast, lunch, and bakery spot.

10. Cucurucho

G2 Río Nazas 52, Cuauhtémoc cucuruchocafe.com • $

Cucurucho is a small chain of cafés inspired by Australian coffee and brunch culture and Japanese hospitality, featuring Mexican beans. Drip, siphon, and pour-over are just a few of the brewing styles offered to customers.

El Ángel (Monumento a la Independencia), soaring above Paseo de la Reforma

CHAPULTEPEC AND POLANCO

The beautiful Bosque de Chapultepec – Latin America's largest urban park – dominates this part of the city. Its shady lawns, bike trails, and lakes provide respite from the city bustle, and a clutch of world-class museums and restaurants make it a favorite weekend recreational spot for locals. Nearby Polanco, on the park's northern edge, is one of Mexico City's most upscale neighborhoods, home to high-end stores and fine-dining restaurants.

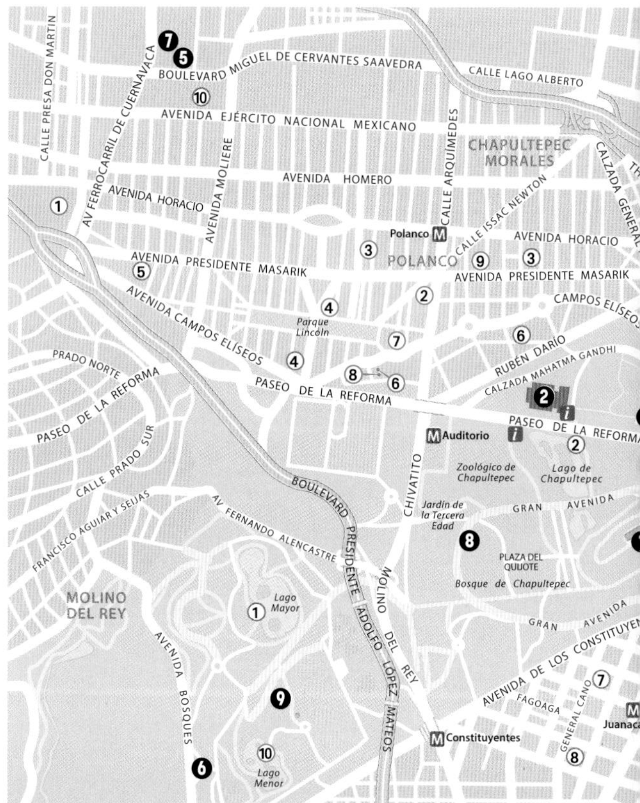

For places to stay in this area, see p132

1 Castillo de Chapultepec

E4 Section 1, Bosque de Chapultepe 9am–4:30pm Tue–Sun mnh.inah.gob.mx

Located atop the highest point in the Bosque de Chapultepec *(p36)*, this castle with its fortress-like walls dominates the Mexico City skyline.

2 Museo Nacional de Antropología

This renowned anthropology museum *(p22)* showcases original artifacts from pre-Hispanic Mexico. The magnificent 180-ton monolith of Tláloc, god of rain, stands near the entrance. Inside, the central courtyard is dominated by a sculpture-fountain called *El Paraguas* (The Umbrella). This 36-ft (11-m), intricately decorated pillar supports a 275-ft- (84-m-) long concrete canopy.

Pyramid of the Feathered Serpent, Museo Nacional de Antropología

3 Museo de Arte Moderno

E3 Paseo de la Reforma and Gandhi, Bosque de Chapultepec 10am–5:30pm Tue–Sun conaculta.gob.mx/mam

Excellent modern paintings, sculpture, and photography from some of the best-known 20th-century Mexican artists are part of the permanent collection housed in this Pedro Ramírez Vásquez- designed building.

4 Museo Rufino Tamayo

E3 Paseo de la Reforma and Gandhi, Bosque de Chapultepec 10am–6pm Tue–Sun museotamayo.org

This collection by internationally recognized modern artists was accumulated by renowned Mexican artist Rufino Tamayo. Tamayo and his wife Olga donated the museum and their collection in 1981.

5 Museo Jumex

B1 Blvd. Miguel de Cervantes Saavedra 303, Granada, Miguel Hidalgo 10am–5pm Tue–Sun (to 7pm Sat) fundacionjumex.org

Since its opening in 2013, Museo Jumex has been an important museum for contemporary art, both Mexican and international. One of its famous exhibits is "Damien Hirst: To Live Forever (For a While)," which drew thousands of visitors.

6 Museo de Historia Natural

B6 Section 2, Bosque de Chapultepec 10am–5pm Tue–Sun sma.df.gob.mx/mhn

The displays of this museum are ideal for children to learn about the natural world. A small planetarium offers exhibits on the creation of the universe, the solar system, and earth. A dinosaur skeleton dominates the center of the Evolution of Life Hall. Three stuffed polar bears are the highlights of the Life on Earth Hall. There is also a section on the Natural History of Mexico.

7 Museo Soumaya

B1 Blvd. Miguel de Cervantes Saavedra, Granada, Miguel Hidalgo 10:30am–6:30pm Wed, Thu, Sun & Mon, 10:30am–8:30pm Fri & Sat soumaya.com.mx

This private museum houses one of the country's most outstanding collections of European, Mexican, and pre-Columbian art. There are also some fine sculptures such as the *Burghers of Calais*, *The Kiss*, *Eve*, and *The Eternal Spring*. Other collections include stunning 18th- and 19th-century Mexican portraits, some contemporary art, and works by international artists such as Edgar Degas, Paul Gauguin, and Camille Claudelle. The museum also displays temporary exhibits by renowned Mexican and international artists.

8 Bosque de Chapultepec

One of the largest, prettiest, and most visited urban parks in the world, the Bosque de Chapultepec *(p36)* is loved by Mexicans and visitors alike. Many visitors come across the park while visiting the Museo Nacional de Antropología or the spectacular hilltop Castillo de Chapultepec which houses the Museo Nacional de Historia. The park offers miles of paved walkways that lead through dense woods, past lakes, into lovely lush gardens, and connect to many more significant museums and attractions. There are lakeside restaurants, picnic spots with tall, shady trees, shops, and places to rent paddleboats.

VOLADORES DE PAPANTLA

The flying men from Veracruz present their traditional ritual dance ceremony near the entrance to the Museo Nacional de Antropología *(p22)*. Five men climb to the top of a 75-ft (23-m) pole. As one plays music and dances, the other four take turns to gracefully slide off the platform with a rope tied to one leg, gradually swirling upside down until each reaches the ground.

Cacti in Jardín Botánico in Bosque de Chapultepec

9 Fuente de Tláloc

C5 Section 2, Bosque de Chapultepec

Designed by Diego Rivera in 1952, the Fuente de Tláloc is a whimsical multihued horizontal mosaic sculpture of a running Tláloc, the Aztec god of rain. A favorite with children, the fountain spreads in front of a small building called El Cárcamo that was once part of the city's water system. Inside, Diego Rivera painted huge murals with beautiful flowing designs venerating water and the workers who built the system that brings water into Mexico City.

10 Monumento a los Niños Héroes

E4 Section 2, Bosque de Chapultepec

This striking monument was made by architect Enrique Aragón and sculptor Ernesto Tamariz out of Carrara marble. Located at the main entrance to the Bosque de Chapultepec (*p36*), it pays tribute to six young cadets who fought valiantly during the US invasion of 1847, defying orders to retreat. Legend says that the last cadet standing wrapped the Mexican flag around himself and jumped off the castle to prevent the Americans from capturing the flag.

Striking architecture of the Museo Soumaya

A DAY IN CHAPULTEPEC

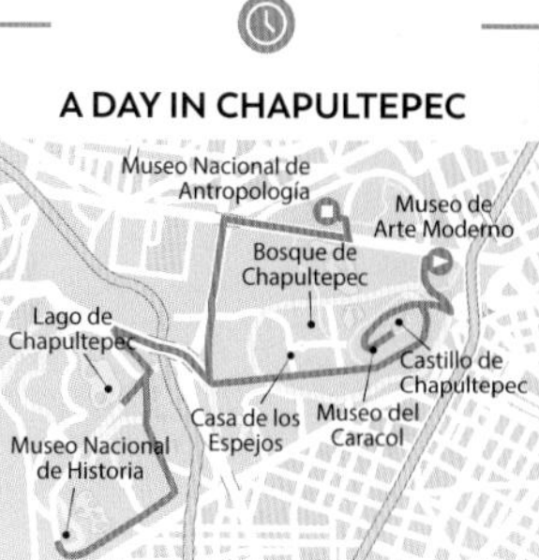

Morning

To the right of the entrance to the **Bosque de Chapultepec** (*p36*) is the **Museo de Arte Moderno** (*p101*). Turn left on the road that leads up to the **Castillo de Chapultepec** (*p101*). When you reach the **Casa de los Espejos** (*p38*) take a tram to the top of the hill. The road curves past the **Museo del Caracol** (*p38*), which highlights major moments in Mexican history. At the top of the hill, enter the Castillo and go to the **Alcázar Section** of the **Museo Nacional de Historia** (*p38*). Explore **President's Mansion**, walk up the **Staircase of the Lions**, and visit the **Garden of the Keep** (*p38*). Head back to the museum's **Castillo Section** (*p38*) and look at the murals before visiting the gift shop.

Afternoon

Descend the hill and follow a sidewalk lined with many vendors – you may want to buy a cold drink – to **Lago de Chapultepec** (*p37*). Turn right toward the **Museo Nacional de Antropología** (*p22*) and follow the signs. After you enter the museum, go into the courtyard and turn left down the stairs for lunch in the excellent café. Spend the rest of the day exploring the fabulous halls of this renowned anthropological museum. Be sure to see the **Mexica Hall** (*p24*) at the end of the courtyard, and the **Teotihuacán Hall** (*p22*).

Excellent book collection at the Librería Porrúa

Shops and Galleries

1. Librería Porrúa

E3 Av. Grutas S/N, Bahía Grutas, Bosque de Chapultepec, Section I porrua.mx

This outpost of the famous bookstore chain has a good collection of books on Mexican art, flora, and fauna.

2. Galería Oscar Román

C3 Calle Julio Verne 14, Polanco Sun galeriaoscarroman.mx

Contemporary Mexican art is on display at this gallery, which has featured shows by sculptor Javier Marín and Neo-Surrealist Laura Quintanilla.

3. Onora

D2 Lope de Vega 330, Polanco onoracasa.com

A homeware boutique, Onora offers superb artisanal crafts. The ceramics and textiles are exceptional.

4. Galería 526

A2 Av. Pdte. Masaryk 526, Polanco Mon seminariode culturamexicana.com

Explore contemporary art by Mexican and international artists at this gallery. It also hosts talks and workshops.

5. LagoAlgo

B5 Pista El Sope s/n, Bosque de Chapultepec, Section II lago-algo.mx

This cultural center showcases art and also houses a lovely restaurant. There's an on-site book and gift shop as well.

6. Plaza Antara

B1 Av. Ejército Nacional Mexicano 843-B, Granada antara.com.mx

Plaza Antara mall features major brands, a spacious play area, a movie theater, and even art installations.

7. Galería RGR

E5 Calle General Antonio León 48, San Miguel Chapultepec Sun rgrart.com

Opened in 2018, this gallery focuses on op-art and kinetic and abstract work, much of it playing with light and intense color.

8. Sala de Arte Público Siqueiros

D3 Calle 3 Picos 29, Polanco Mon saps-latallera.org

This space preserves the work and ideas of artist Davíd Álvaro Siqueiros.

9. Galería Enrique Guerrero

E5 Calle General Juan Cano 103, San Miguel Chapultepec Sun galeriaenriqueguerrero.com

Artworks in multiple media can be seen at this gallery, such as sculptures, photos, videos, and other digital works.

10. Art House

E3 Rincón del Bosque 43, Bosque de Chapultepec, Section I Sun arthousemx.com

An up-and-coming gallery, Art House showcases "ultra-contemporary" works by local and international artists.

Places to Eat

1. Hacienda de los Morales

A2 Vázquez de Mella 525, Del Bosque haciendadelosmorales.com · $$

Enjoy international and Mexican dining in a lovely 16th-century hacienda. For dinner, the dress code for men is casual elegant with a jacket and collared shirt.

2. Quintonil

D2 Av. Isaac Newton 55, Polanco Sun quintonil.com · $$$

One of the best restaurants in Polanco, Quintonil offers a tasting menu of seasonal Mexican dishes. Book ahead.

3. Pujol

C2 Tennyson 133 Sun pujol.com.mx · $$$

Visit this stylish restaurant for dishes such as ceviche in coconut milk and fish cooked in ashes of *chile ancho* (ripened and dried poblano peppers).

4. Bello Puerto

C2 Julio Verne 89, Polanco bellopuerto.com · $$

Reasonable prices, colorful beach decor, and lively music draw a young crowd to this seafood restaurant.

5. Los Panchos

F3 Tolstoi 9, Anzures lospanchos.us · $

This popular restaurant near the park specializes in *carnitas* (roast pork). It is also worth trying the handmade tortillas, the salsas, and the *aguas frescas* (fresh fruit drinks).

6. Au Pied de Cochon

C3 Campos Elíseos 218, Polanco aupieddecochon.com.mx · $$

Sublime French cuisine is served round the clock at this bistro in the Presidente InterContinental Hotel. Booking ahead is advisable.

PRICE CATEGORIES

For a three-course meal for one, with half a bottle of wine (or equivalent meal), taxes, and extra charges.

$ under $300 $$ $300–$650
$$$ over $650

7. Agua & Sal

C3 Campos Elíseos 199-A, Polanco aguaysal.com.mx · $$

The menu at this popular seafood restaurant is inspired by Caribbean and South American cuisine.

8. Chapulin

C3 Campos Elíseos 218, Polanco chapulin.rest · $$$

Upscale Mexican dining featuring local delicacies, including *chapulines*, *chicatanas*, and *escamoles* *(p75)*.

9. Rincón Argentino

D2 Av. Presidente Masarik 177, Polanco rinconargentino.com · $$

Large platters of excellent beef are grilled to order. The decor is casual Argentina ranch.

10. Del Bosque Restaurante

B6 Lago Mayor, Section 2, Bosque de Chapultepec delbosquerestaurante.com.mx · $$

This pet-friendly restaurant offers an extensive menu featuring breakfast options along with Mexican specialties.

Salsa verde with cucumber and mint at Pujol

SAN ÁNGEL AND COYOACÁN

Once pastoral suburbs on the outskirts of Mexico City, San Ángel and Coyoacán are part of the main city today, but nonetheless manage to retain a small-town feel. These tranquil suburban enclaves were favored by artists and writers in the 20th century, including Frida Kahlo, Diego Rivera, and Leon Trotsky, whose former homes and studios have been turned into fascinating museums. Adding to the charm are cobbled streets lined with cafés, boutiques, and canals.

1 Plaza Hidalgo

U2 Calles Carrillo Puerto, Caballo Calco and B. Domínguez,

At one end of this lively plaza stands the Iglesia de San Juan Bautista. The church's elegant interior features an ornate 17th-century Baroque altarpiece. Murals depicting local history are in the attached chapel. At the other end is the 16th-century Casa de Cortés – Mexico's first municipal seat – home to several government offices. Across the Calle Carrillo Felipe Puerto is the Jardín del Centenario *(p66)* and the famous Fountain of Coyoacán.

2 Museo Nacional de las Intervenciones

U1 Calle 20 de Agosto s/n, San Diego Churubusco 9am–4pm Tue–Sat lugares.inah.gob.mx

Museo Nacional de las Intervenciones is located within a former convent,

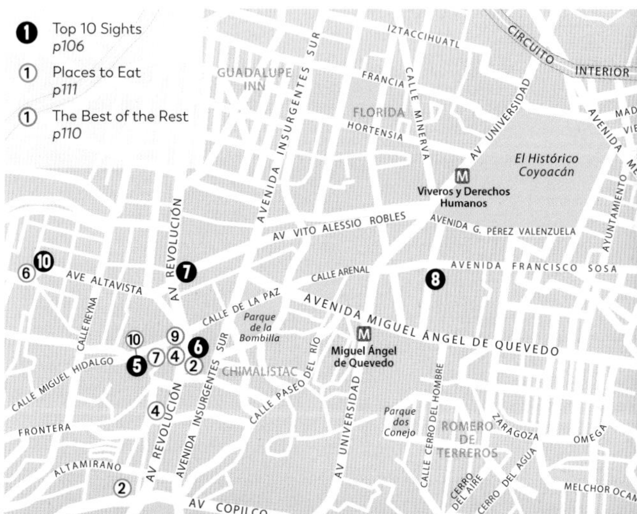

For places to stay in this area, see p133

El Antiguo Convento Churubusco. It chronicles the invasions of Mexico following its independence from Spain. Highlighted here is the Spanish invasion of 1829, the French invasion of 1838–9, the US invasion of 1846–7, the French invasion of 1862–7, as well as incursions by the US in 1914 and 1916. There are displays of documents, military artifacts, uniforms, and historical narratives from the battles.

3 Museo Anahuacallí

U3 Museo 150, San Pablo Tepetlapah 11am–5:30pm Tue–Sat museoanahuacalli.org

Diego Rivera commissioned the construction of this museum, which was completed after his death by multiple artists, including Rivera's daughter. The museum, built of black volcanic stone, takes the form of a pyramid. It features Rivera's vast collection of pre-Hispanic artifacts, murals, and mosaics. The rooftop terrace offers breathtaking views of the city. The museum often hosts festivals and special events; its Day of the Dead celebrations are spectacular.

Kahlo's vibrant kitchen at the Museo Frida Kahlo

4 Museo Frida Kahlo

This vibrant blue house *(p34)* is where Frida Kahlo was born and spent most of her life creating her greatest works. A self-taught painter, she developed a unique style here that blended realist and surrealist elements. The house is filled with personal belongings, paintings, and the favorite artworks of Kahlo and her husband, Diego Rivera. Kahlo's studio has her easel and paintbrushes, the bedroom displays her signature Mexican regional clothing and jewelry, and the cheery kitchen is filled with Mexican pottery.

5 El Bazaar Sábado

Q3 Plaza San Jacinto 11 10am–7pm Sat bazaarsabado.com

This festive Saturday-only shopping event is housed in an old colonial mansion. Dozens of beautifully adorned booths displaying exquisite decorative and functional art fill the rooms around the courtyard. Intricate silver jewelry, papier-mâché figures, hand-embroidered clothing, hand-carved and painted woodwork, and ceramics are on offer. The mansion's courtyard is home to the popular Restaurante Oxa *(p111)*.

6 Ex-Convento e Iglesia del Carmen

Q3 Av. Revolución 4, San Ángel 10am–5pm Tue–Sun 5616-1504

Built for Carmelite monks in the 17th century, this church has three beautiful mosaic-tiled domes. A basement crypt, found in 1914, contains the mummified bodies of priests, nuns, and nobility. On the top floor is a chapel with a Baroque altar. The adjacent Museo del Carmen *(p110)* has displays on religious art. A separate entry fee is charged for visiting the museum (except on Sundays).

7 Museo de Arte Carrillo Gil

Q2 Av. Revolución 1608 10am–6pm Tue–Sun museodeartecarrillogil.com

The museum's permanent collection of early 20th-century Mexican masters includes paintings by José Clemente Orozco, David Alfaro Siqueiros, Diego Rivera, Gunther Gerzso, Wolfgang Paalen, and others. The collection was assembled by Dr. Álvar and Carmen Carrillo Gil and is housed in a bright, modern three-story building. The museum is noted for its exceptional temporary exhibits featuring Mexican and international contemporary art.

8 Museo Nacional de la Acuarela

S2 Salvador Novo 88 10am–6pm daily acuarela.org.mx

This internationally renowned museum was founded by celebrated artist Alfredo Guati Rojo and his wife. Set in a large two-story house with a pretty garden, it has a permanent exhibit on the history of watercolor in Mexico, an international section, and galleries featuring contemporary Mexican art. Works by the likes of Pastor Velázquez, Manuel M. Ituarte, Leandro Izaguirre, and Eduardo Solares adorn the gallery walls. Two outstanding canvases are *La Carrera del Fuego* and *Jazz*, both by Ángel Mauro Rodríguez, on display on the first floor.

9 Cineteca Nacional

T1 Av. México Coyoacán 389, Xoco 9am–10:30pm Mon–Fri, 10am–10:30pm Sat & Sun cinetecanacional.net

Mexico's eminent national cinema, the Cineteca Nacional is a sprawling campus

LA MALINCHE

Mystery surrounds La Malinche, the enslaved Maya woman who was Cortés' translator and trusted negotiator. She played a key role during the conquest of the Aztec empire, serving as the link between the Spaniards and the Indigenous cultures that occupied the area at the time. She lived in Coyoacán with Cortés' son, and their child is considered the first *mestizo*.

Museo del Carmen in the Ex-Convento e Iglesia del Carmen

dedicated to preserving, studying, and promoting both Mexican and international cinema. The complex includes ten theaters where regular screenings are held, an outdoor screen for open-air movie nights, and a gallery housing film-related exhibits. There's also a vast archive and a digital restoration lab on the property, and many food stalls and cafés. Check the website for information on screenings, special features, and academic events.

10 Museo Casa Estudio Diego Rivera y Frida Kahlo

P2 Calle Diego Rivera and Altavista For renovation, check website inba.gob.mx/recinto/51

Built by fellow muralist, friend, and architect Juan O'Gorman in 1931–2, this site has two buildings joined by a second-floor walkway. The larger white studio was Diego Rivera's, where he painted many of his best-known oils. This space has been perfectly preserved, with some of the paintings still standing on easels. The smaller blue studio was Frida Kahlo's when she lived here with Rivera. It is here that she created some of her most famous works, *What the Water Gave Me*, *The Watchful Eye*, and *The Deceased Dimas*.

Exterior of the Museo Casa Estudio Diego Rivera y Frida Kahlo

A STROLL THROUGH COYOACÁN

Morning

Begin at the **Museo Nacional de la Acuarela**, located on Salvador Novo, south of Avenida Francisco Sosa. After viewing the watercolors, walk back to **Avenida Francisco Sosa** along one of the prettiest cobblestone streets of Coyoacán, with its old colonial mansions and the charming yellow Church of Santa Catarina. Cross the street into the garden of the cultural center, Casa de la Cultura Jesús Reyes Heroles *(No. 202)*. Farther along is the **Jardín del Centenario** *(p66)*. View the Fountain of Coyoacán. Move to the adjacent **Plaza Hidalgo** *(p107)* and admire the interior of the Iglesia de San Juan Bautista. Explore the area around the plaza. Lunch at trendy **Los Danzantes** *(p111)*.

Afternoon

Head north on Allende for three blocks to **Mercado de Coyoacán** *(p72)* and soak in the sights, sounds, and smells in this pretty market where colorful arrays of fresh fruits and vegetables, piñatas, toys, and crafts are on sale amid the tantalizing smell of Mexican food. Carry on to Londres to visit the **Museo Frida Kahlo** *(p34)* where the famous artist was born, lived, and painted. Head back to Plaza Hidalgo for some of Coyoacán's renowned ice cream at **Helados Siberia** *(p111)*.

The Best of the Rest

1. Tlacuilo

U3 Europa 13, Barrio de la Concepción By appointment only

Artist Pedro Reyes' private library features floor-to-ceiling bookshelves. It is also home to his studio.

2. Museo del Carmen

Q3 Av. Revolución 4, San Ángel sic.gob.mx

Founded as a Carmelite monastery in 1615, this convent was converted into a museum in 1938.

3. Museo Casa de León Trotsky

U1 Av. Río Churubusco 410 museotrotsky.org.mx

Leon Trotsky sought refuge in this house while he was in exile and lived here until he was assassinated in 1940.

4. Centro Cultural San Ángel

C3 Av. Revolución s/n, San Ángel

Set in a 19th-century building, this cultural center is home to the Teatro López Tarso, which stages various plays in Spanish.

5. CENART

U1 Av. Río Churubusco 79, Coyoacán cenart.gob.mx

CENART's huge campus is home to galleries, concert and theater spaces, and hosts cultural events.

6. Centro Cultural Elena Garro

U2 Fernández Leal 43, Coyoacán educal.com.mx/elenagarro

With a floor-to-ceiling wall of glass around the exterior, this cultural center has an inviting garden and café.

7. Museo Casa del Risco

Q3 Plaza San Jacinto 5, San Ángel museocasadelrisco.org.mx

This museum's ultra-Baroque fountain features remarkable ceramic work.

8. Coyoacán's Tranvía Turístico Trolley

T2 Jardín Plaza Hidalgo, Coyoacán 5658-4027

The Tranvía Turístico trolley will take you to nine key sights in Coyoacán.

9. Mercado del Carmen

Q3 Calle de la Amargura 5, San Ángel mncp.cultura.gob.mx

This modern food hall features more than 30 stalls and boutiques selling perfume, books, and other accessories.

10. Museo Nacional de Culturas Populares

U2 Av. Miguel Hidalgo 289, Coyoacán mncp.cultura.gob.mx

Find Mexican arts and crafts here. Check the website for special events, like the tamale fair and ice cream festival.

Traditional pottery, Museo Nacional de Culturas Populares

Places to Eat

Patrons enjoying a meal at the Restaurante Oxa

PRICE CATEGORIES

For a three-course meal for one, with half a bottle of wine (or equivalent meal), taxes, and extra charges.

$ under $300 $$ $300–$650
$$$ over $650

1. Helados Siberia

U2 Plaza Jardín del Centenario 3, Coyoacán • $

This legendary ice-cream shop has an excellent selection of flavors.

2. Taberna de León

Q3 Altamirano 46, Plaza Loreto, San Ángel 5616-3951 Sun dinner • $$$

Chef Monica Patiño prepares Mexican and international specialties in this romantic restaurant located in a converted paper factory.

3. Cantina La Coyoacana

U2 Higuera 14, Coyoacán 5658-5337 Mon–Sat • $

This traditional family cantina serves Mexican specialties in a c. 1932 mansion with an antique bar, stained-glass windows, and a great ambience.

4. Fonda San Ángel

Q3 Plaza San Jacinto 3, San Ángel fondasanangel.com.mx • $$

Mexican specialties with exceptional sauces are served in this cozy restaurant.

5. Entrevero

T2 Jardín del Centenario 14-C, Coyoacán 5659-0066 • $$

Entrevero is an attractive and informal bistro serving Uruguayan specialties.

6. Los Danzantes

U2 Plaza Jardín del Centenario 12, Coyoacán losdanzantes.com • $$

Dine at this stylish, intimate restaurant for contemporary Mexican fusion cuisine with Oaxacan flavors and a creative twist.

7. San Ángel Inn

P2 Diego Rivera 50, San Ángel sanangelinn.com • $$$

Housed in an old Carmelite monastery, this fine restaurant offers both formal and casual dining.

8. Corazón de Maguey

U2 Jardín del Centenario 9A, Coyoacán Fri corazondemaguey.com • $$$

Enjoy contemporary Mexican dishes and an extensive mezcal menu here. If you're interested in seasonal Mexican delicacies, ask for the *tacos de gusanos de maguey*, made with a worm that lives in the maguey plant.

9. Masiosare

T3 Felipe Carrillo Puerto 50, Coyoacán 5086-3381 • $$$

Masiosare is a modern take on the classic cantina. It has a great selection of mezcal and tequila. Regulars love the variety of live music and DJ sets, which range from African beats to salsa.

10. Restaurante Oxa

P3 Plaza San Jacinto 13, San Ángel oxa.com.mx • $$

This café is housed in the courtyard of El Bazaar de Sábado *(p107)*.

Clockwise from above **Fountain of Coyoacán in the pretty Jardín del Centenario; the bright-yellow town hall in Coyoacán; Iglesia de San Juan Bautista's interior**

GREATER MEXICO CITY

Beyond the traditional center, Mexico City extends into the surrounding valleys and high plateaus, where interesting neighborhoods, archaeological sites, and national parks await. Visitors can cruise along the floating gardens of Xochimilco, ride a *cablebús* over the rooftops of Iztapalapa, or take a day trip to the ancient pyramids of Teotihuacán – all within easy reach of the capital by bus and taxi.

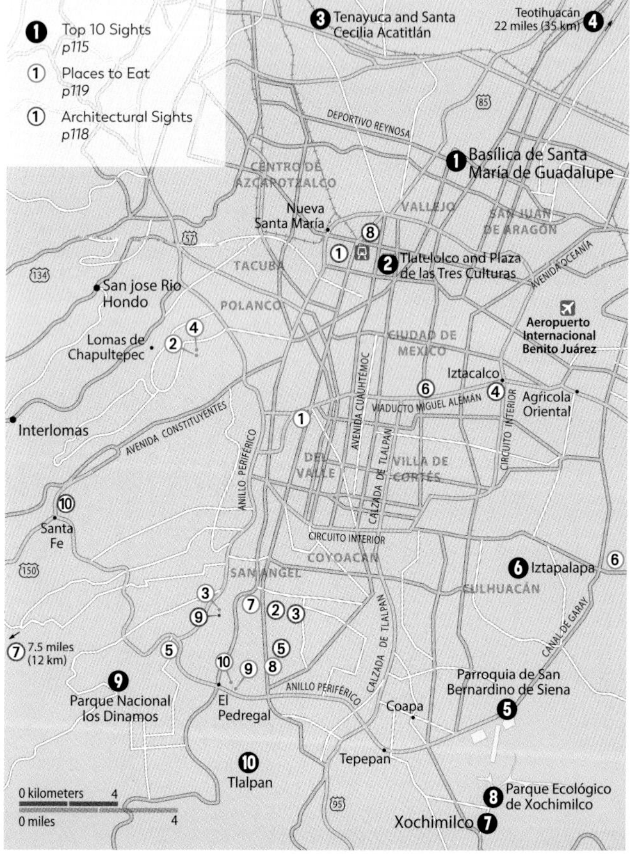

For places to stay in this area, see p133

1 Basílica de Santa María de Guadalupe

Mexico's holiest Catholic shrine *(p44)* is dedicated to Our Lady of Guadalupe, the beautiful dark-skinned image of the Virgin that appeared to Juan Diego in 1531 and left an imprint of her image on his *tilma* (a traditional cloak made of cactus fibers). The *tilma* is displayed in the Nueva Basílica. There are many chapels, basilicas, and holy sites here, each one commemorating an aspect of this holy site. The Basílica Antigua, with its elaborately decorated Baroque facade and twin towers, housed the image of Guadalupe from 1709 until the Nueva Basílica was consecrated in 1976.

2 Tlatelolco and Plaza de las Tres Culturas

X2 Eje Central & Ricardo Flores Magón Ruins: 9am–6pm Tue–Sun

Tlatelolco was once the site of the largest Aztec commercial trading center. The Spanish destroyed the ancient Aztec palaces, temples, and ceremonial center, making way for the plaza and the Church of Santiago. Much of the ruins, including the main pyramid with its twin temples, have been excavated. Modern buildings surround the plaza, giving rise to its name, which means "plaza of three cultures," after the unique blend of Aztec, colonial, and modern-era structures that can be seen here.

Remains of Tlatelolco with the Church of Santiago

3 Tenayuca and Santa Cecilia Acatitlán

W1 10 miles (17 km) N of Mexico City 10am–4:30pm Tue–Sun

These two ancient pyramids located near each other in the north of Mexico City make it possible to visit both archaeological sites in a single taxi trip. The oldest, Tenayuca, was built in the 11th century before the Aztecs arrived in the valley. The pyramid was enlarged every 52 years, six times in all, and twin staircases lead to the temples on the top. The second pyramid, Santa Cecilia Acatitlán, dates from 1300–1521, and was used to worship the sun god Huitzilopochtli and the rain god Tláloc. The temple at the top of the pyramid has been carefully and authentically reconstructed, and visitors can climb the staircase to explore the historic building.

4 Teotihuacán

This is not the only archaeological site *(p46)* in or around Mexico City, but it is the largest, most accessible, and most frequently visited one. While visitors can no longer climb the huge pyramids here, they are no less impressive to view from the surrounds.

5 Parroquia de San Bernardino de Siena

X4 Pino and Violeta, Xochimilco

Flower-filled gardens surround this graceful church. Ornate doorways lead to one of Mexico's last surviving 16th-century altarpieces. This magnificent *retablo* has paintings by Baltazar de Echave and sculptures by Luis de Arciniega. A unique feature of this church is the row of pre-Hispanic skulls mounted on the side walls, with a sign reminding parishioners how to make a good confession.

6 Iztapalapa

Y3 11 miles (18 km) S of Mexico City

While Iztapalapa attracts fewer visitors than other sites around Mexico City, it has much to offer. One of the attractions in this outlying suburb is the Línea 2 *cablebús*, which covers 6.5 miles (10.5 km). It holds the Guinness World Record for being the longest cable car in Latin America. The cabins glide over densely packed neighborhoods where the rooftops feature colorful, large-scale murals. It takes about 45 minutes to ride the full circuit, which also travels over the Sierra de Santa Catarina mountain range. Near the boarding station is the fascinating Museo Yancuic, an interactive museum, which opened in 2024. The museum is designed to teach children about biodiversity and climate change.

7 Xochimilco

Popular with both locals and tourists, many come to the floating gardens of Xochimilco *(p42)* to glide leisurely in *trajineras* (flat-bottomed barges) through the shallow waters of the ancient Aztec canals, lined with flower-festooned nurseries and homes. The barges are available for rent by the hour.

8 Parque Ecológico de Xochimilco

X4 Anillo Periférico 1, Ciénega Grande

This 740-acre (300-hectare) park was created to help preserve and maintain Xochimilco's canals and floating gardens and is protected by UNESCO. Several scenic walking paths curve through the park. *Trajineras* provide boat trips through the natural areas to see native and cultivated flora, as well

CHINAMPAS

The Xochimilcas devised a unique method of farming. They built rafts with bark and reeds, piled lake mud onto them and then planted trees with a deep root system. As the trees grew, the rafts were anchored to the lake bed. These *chinampas*, or floating gardens, thrived – growing many crops and flowers. After the Spanish conquest, Xochimilco was spared from destruction as it was the main source of food for the city.

Colorful *trajineras* on a canal in Xochimilco

as various species of birds here. There is also a visitor center, a museum, and educational shows that explain how the impressive floating islands were built.

9 Parque Nacional los Dinamos

W4 Magdalena Contreras
9am–5pm daily

Popular with nature lovers, this wooded expanse borders the ravine of the Magdalena River. Favorite activities here include walking, hiking, and biking. Horses are often available for hire on weekends and holidays, and there are plenty of picnic spots. The park also offers the best rock climbing in the area, with walls of varying difficulty reaching as high as 100 ft (30 m). There are several different rock formations requiring a variety of climbing techniques. Weekends and holidays are the best time to visit. If you plan to explore the less-frequented areas of the park it is advisable that you first speak with one of the park's rangers.

10 Tlalpan

W4 Mex 95, 15 miles (25 km) S of Mexico City

In the age of the Spanish viceroys, Tlalpan was a favorite country retreat for both ordinary Mexicans and the nobility. As a result, a large number of elegant mansions and haciendas were built here from the early 18th century onward. Visitors to the old town can stroll along narrow streets and admire the beautiful architecture. The central Plaza de la Constitución features the Capilla del Rosario, an 18th-century chapel with a Baroque facade. In the same square stands the tree from which 11 patriots, who rebelled against the French occupation under Emperor Maximilian I, were hanged in 1866. At the corner of San Fernando and Madero is the former country house of General Antonio López de Santa Anna, the victor of the Battle of the Alamo. He was named president of Mexico 11 times.

A DAY IN GREATER MEXICO CITY

Morning

Start your day with a visit to the **Basílica de Santa María de Guadalupe** *(p115)* – an architectural wonder and pilgrimage site. Then, head across Plaza Mariana to the **Museo de la Basílica de Santa María de Guadalupe** *(p44)*, which displays some of the unusual offerings left at the church by worshipers.

Afternoon

In the afternoon, take the metro, metrobús, or a taxi or car service 4 miles (6 km) south to the **Tlatelolco** archeological site *(p115)*. Spend some time exploring the **Plaza de las Tres Culturas** *(p115)*, a complex reminder of Mexico's long history: the remains here are pre-Hispanic; the church is from the colonial period; and the buildings, designed by architect Mario Pani, represent the modern era.

Next, make your way to the **Centro Cultural Universitario Tlatelolco** *(Av. Ricardo Flores Magón 1)*, a cultural center that hosts art exhibits, lectures, and workshops on the area's history. After this, head to **Mirador Tlatelolco** *(Av. Paeso de la Reforma 716)*, a private art gallery located on the 24th floor of one of Pani's apartments. End the day with dinner at chef Gabriela Cámara's **Caracol de Mar** *(República de Guatemala 20)*, known for its delectable Mexican and Peruvian seafood.

Architectural Sights

1. Kiosco Morisco

W2 Jaime Torres Bodet 152, Santa María la Ribera

This Neo-Mudejar kiosk dates to 1884 and is made entirely of wrought iron, with the exception of its glass cupola.

2. Biblioteca Central de la UNAM

W3 Escolar, Ciudad Universitaria

The mosaic covering the university's main library depicts pre-Hispanic and Mexican history, with the fourth wall a tribute to the university itself.

3. Facultad de Medicina UNAM

W3 Escolar 411A, Copilco Universidad

The mosaic on Building A at UNAM's School of Medicine represents indigenous cosmology.

4. Palacio de los Deportes

X3 Av. Viaducto Río de la Piedad at Río Churubusco, Granjas

Architect Félix Candela created this "Sports Palace" for the 1968 Olympics.

5. Espacio Escultórico UNAM

W3 CUT, Mario de La Cueva, Universitaria

This outdoor sculpture rings a field of volcanic rocks and black lava left by the eruption of the Xitle volcano.

6. Biblioteca Vasconcelos

W2 Eje 1 Norte s/n, Buenavista
bibliotecavasconcelos.gob.mx

Inaugurated in 2006, this seven-story-high library has suspended, expandable shelves. It also has a Braille room.

7. Ex Convento Desierto de los Leones

V4 Carretera Toluca, Cuajimalpa de Morelos 9131-9542 Mon

This 17th-century convent was built in the forest, far from the city, for the Carmelite order to meditate in silence.

8. Torre Insignia

X2 Torre Insignia, Tlatelolco

Also known as Torre Banobras, this skyscraper was one of the city's tallest buildings when it was completed in 1962.

9. Tetetlán

W3 Av. de Las Fuentes 180-B, Jardines del Pedregal tetetlan.com

This center has transparent floors, which show the volcanic rock upon which the neighborhood is built.

10. Iglesia San Josemaría Escrivá

V3 Joaquín Gallo 101, Santa Fe
iglesiasanjosemaria.org.mx

Considered a modern architectural masterpiece, this church features an abstract interpretation of core Christian teachings.

Exploring the stunning Kiosco Morisco

Places to Eat

A marinated fish dish and a plate of chicken sandwiches at Nube 7

PRICE CATEGORIES

For a three-course meal for one, with half a bottle of wine (or equivalent meal), taxes, and extra charges.

$ under $300 $$ $300–$650
$$$ over $650

1. Bellini

W3 Montecito 38, 45th floor, Nápoles bellini.com.mx · $$$

Enjoy 360-degree views of the city skyline while dining at Bellini, the world's largest rotating restaurant.

2. Aromas

W2 Monte Everest 770, Lomas de Chapultepec 7313-9072 · $$

A gallery, shop, bakery, and restaurant serving internationally inspired dishes with locally sourced ingredients.

3. Tetetlán

W3 Av. de Las Fuentes 180-B, Jardines del Pedregal tetetlan.com · $$

A favorite among locals and visitors alike, this restaurant specializes in contemporary Mexican cuisine.

4. Casa Ó

W2 Monte Líbano 245, Lomas de Chapultepec 5520-9227 · $$

French techniques meet Mexican ingredients at this upscale bistro where local business people seal deals over dishes like pappardelle with short rib.

5. Restaurante Forno di Casa

W3 Desierto de los Leones 5525, Colonia Alcantarilla 1520-5785 · $$

This Italian restaurant is an ideal option near Desierto de los Leones, with pasta made fresh daily on site.

6. Mariscos 7 Mares

X3 Av. San Rafael Atlixco 3, Colonia Guadalupe del Moral · $

It's not fancy, but this popular spot has over 100 fish and "fruit of the sea" dishes, including stews and aguachiles.

7. Restaurante Casa Club del Académico

W3 Av Cd Universitaria 301, Ciudad Universitaria 1520-5785 · $

This family-friendly place features entertainment for kids and gardens that include a hydroponic greenhouse.

8. Nube 7

W3 Insurgentes Sur 3000, Ciudad Universitaria nube7.mx · $

Located inside MUAC *(p62)*, this is an ideal option if you're hungry while visiting UNAM's attractions. Both the food and atmosphere are unfussy.

9. Sud 777

W3 Blvd. de la Luz 777, Jardines de Pedregal sud777.com.mx · $$$

Discover why Chef Edgar Nuñez's contemporary Mexican restaurant has landed a spot on Latin America's 50 Best Restaurants list four years in a row. There is also a tasting menu for vegans, as well.

10. Cortile Pedregal

W3 Cráter 823, Jardines del Pedregal 7602-1306 · $$

The menu here leans Italian, but you'll also see Mexican ingredients and plates such as stuffed squash blossoms. Don't skip the artful cocktails or desserts, which are all beautifully presented.

STREETSMART

Tacos served with lime and salsa

GETTING AROUND

Whether you're exploring Mexico City by foot or making use of public transportation, here is everything you need to know to navigate the city and the areas beyond the center like a pro.

AT A GLANCE

PUBLIC TRANSPORTATION

METRO

$5

One-way journey

METROBÚS

$6

One-way journey

CABLEBÚS

$7

One-way journey

TOP TIP

Purchase a MI card to use all of Mexico City's transportation systems.

SPEED LIMIT

URBAN ZONE FREEWAYS

50 km/h (30 mph)

RESIDENTIAL STREETS

30 km/h (15 mph)

HIGHWAYS OUTSIDE THE CITY

80 km/h (50 mph)

Arriving by Air

Two major airports service Mexico City. Most visitors will arrive at Benito Juárez International Airport, which is more commonly known as Aeropuerto Internacional de la Ciudad de México (MEX). Located 3 miles (5 km) east of downtown Mexico City, this airport is the closest to the city center. It has two terminals, which are connected by a free shuttle, and has the most easily accessible transportation options, including the Metro, taxis, and car services. Metro Line 5 (yellow) connects the airport with the city center; follow signs for the Metro at Terminal 1. Taxi ranks can be found on exiting the arrivals level of either terminal. Fares are indicated by zone and are paid in advance of the ride.

The second airport is Aeropuerto Internacional Felipe Ángeles (NLU), also known as AIFA. It is located 20 miles (35 km) north of the city center. While flights into and out of NLU tend to be less expensive than MEX, transportation to and from the city center can be more challenging to navigate, with the main options being taxis and van services. The Tren Suburbano (suburban rail) is scheduled to begin operating from NLU in late 2024 and will connect to the city center in around 30 minutes.

Long-distance Bus Travel

Mexico has a number of bus providers, and bus travel from Mexico City to points beyond is safe, comfortable, and affordable. Popular lines include **ADO**, **ETN**, **Estrella Roja**, **Futura**, and **Omnibus**. Tickets are available online and at the four major bus terminals in the city: Terminal del Norte, Terminal del Sur (Tasqueña), Terminal del Oriente, and Central del Poniente (Observatorio).

ADO
W ado.com.mx

Estrella Roja
W estrellaroja.com.mx

ETN
W etn.com.mx
Futura
W futura.com.mx
Omnibus
W odm.com.mx

Public Transportation

Mexico City's excellent and extensive public transportation is operated by multiple systems. It covers most of the city via Metro, Metrobús, Cablebús, Trolebús, Tren Ligero (light rail), RTP (urban bus service), Tren Suburbano (rail system), and Mexibús. Most visitors are likely to use the Metro, Metrobús, and Cablebús, as the other systems connect to the city's suburbs.

Stations and vehicles are clean and well-maintained, and public safety officers are visible at almost every stop or station. Most transportation runs from 5am to midnight. The first car of all trains in the Metro system and the front area of every Metrobús is reserved for women and children.

Tickets

To travel on any of the transportation systems you can use a contactless credit card, but if this will incur charges, a better option is to buy a MI card, officially called a *Tarjeta Movilidad Integrada* (Integrated Mobility Card). This card costs $21 and can be purchased and reloaded at any Metro or Metrobús station. Hold your contactless credit card or MI card infront of the sensor at the turnstile at stations and stops to access the platform, or scan your card on the sensor as you board the vehicle.

Metro

Mexico City's **Metro** has 12 color-coded lines and covers a large portion of the city and also extends to the suburbs. Each ride on the Metro costs $5. The system runs from 5am to midnight Monday to Friday, from 6am to midnight on Saturdays, and from 7am to midnight on Sundays and public holidays. Before using the Metro, purchase a MI card and load it with funds at a station.
Metro
W metro.cdmx.gob.mx

Metrobús

The **Metrobús** system has seven lines and operates across most of the city. It is a fast and efficient way to get around due to the many designated bus lanes that bypass the traffic. The Metrobús costs $6 per ride and uses the same MI card system as the Metro. Line 7 is particularly useful for visitors as it runs along Paseo de la Reforma passing key sights such as Monumento a la Revolución, Bosque de Chapultepec, and Museo Nacional de Antropología.
Metrobús
W metrobus.cdmx.gob.mx

Cablebús

This cable car system has three lines that glide above the city's congested streets, offering excellent views of Bosque Chapultepec, the Iztapalapa neighborhood in the north, plus the mountains on the city's edge. It costs $7 per ride, and like the Metro and Metrobús, uses the MI card.
Cablebús
W ste.cdmx.gob.mx/cablebus

GETTING TO AND FROM THE AIRPORT

Airport	Transportation	Journey Time	Price
Aeropuerto Internacional Ciudad de México (MEX)	Taxi	15-20 mins	$200-$400
	Metro (Line 5)	45-60 mins	$5
Aeropuerto Internacional Felipe Ángeles (NLU)	Taxi	60 mins	$500-$600
	Tren Suburbano (from late 2024)	30 mins	$120
	EcoElite Van Service	60 mins	$120

Turibus

Mexico City's **Turibus** is a double-decker, hop-on-hop-off bus that runs from 9am to 7pm daily and offers four different routes, all with narration offered in multiple languages. The Turibus is one of the best ways to travel to the city's main attractions and to understand the size, scope, and diversity of Mexico City.

Turibus
W turibus.com.mx

Taxis and Car Services

Public taxis are pink and white and run on a metered system. Uber and similar services (such as Didi, a local alternative) are preferred over taxis for the security they offer, as well as the predictable fare and the ability to pay via credit or debit card. In addition, visitors have reported problems with public taxis, including fare scams that aren't recognized until after a credit card has been charged repeatedly or with an excessive amount.

Driving

Mexico City's public transportation system makes it easy to be without a car, and an extensive bus system connects the capital to all interesting points beyond the city. If you do intend to drive in and around the city, here's what you need to consider.

Driving in Mexico City

Driving in Mexico City can be a hair-raising experience and is best avoided. Dense traffic, multi-lane highways and roads, complex toll road systems, and difficult-to-read signage are among the challenges drivers will experience. Robberies do occur, and it is advisable not to drive at night, and to avoid overnight street parking. In Mexico City, drive with the doors locked and the windows rolled up. Plan your trip in advance, take a good road map, check if your route includes toll roads, and know where your stops are likely to be.

Mexico City controls pollution and traffic density with a program called *Hoy no circula*, which prohibits license plates with certain numbers from traveling in the city on certain days. There are also prohibitions on driving on days when pollution levels exceed a specific threshold. These systems and rules can be confusing, and some public safety officers have been known to attempt to take advantage of any lack of knowledge to impose fines.

Car Rental

International car rental agencies operate branches at the Aeropuerto Internacional de la Ciudad de México airport and at multiple locations in the city. When pre-booking, make sure the price incorporates the 16 percent sales (IVA) tax and full insurance. It is important that the insurance includes theft and collision damage waiver. Some policies provide only nominal coverage (liability insurance is the minimal legal requirement), and you may need to pay for additional insurance coverage. If your credit card company covers international rentals, be sure to bring documentation to that effect. Before leaving the car rental lot, make sure that the vehicle is in good condition, has valid insurance and registration documents in the glove compartment, and confirm procedures for any roadside assistance or emergencies.

To rent a car in Mexico you must be 21 or over (25 for some agencies) and have held a driver's license for at least one year. The rental must be paid for with a major credit card.

It is unlikely that you will be rented a car with license plates from Mexico City or from Estado de México, but if your car has either, be sure to ask about circulation regulations. Be aware that many rental car agencies attempt to impose unnecessary, excessive fees, including insurance that is not required, on unsuspecting drivers, so be knowledgeable about your existing coverage and firm in your communication about that coverage.

Parking

Parking is abundant throughout the city, both streetside and in private lots and garages. Parking is permitted where you see a sign with an E (for *estacionamiento*) in a circle. The same E with a diagonal line through it means no parking. A white E on a blue background indicates a parking lot.

Rates are reasonable, though are often charged in local currency (debit or credit cards are not accepted), so ask before parking about rates and terms of payment. Many parking spaces in residential and commercial zones are pay-by-meter. While affordable, these are monitored closely by transportation officials, who won't hesitate to put an *araña*, or "spider," lock on your car's wheel if you fail to pay or exceed your paid parking time. Pay close attention to signage indicating valid parking hours and rate details, and be sure to not let your meter expire.

Rules of the Road

All drivers are legally required to carry a valid driver's license and registration and insurance documents. Foreign visitors are also likely to be asked to produce a passport or, if applicable, residency documents.

Drive on the right. Many streets are one way. The city has few stop signs, but many traffic lights. Seat belts are mandatory for all passengers. Distances are measured in kilometers rather than miles, and gas is sold in liters. Mexican gas stations have staff who pump the gas for you (motorists are not allowed to do this themselves); they will often offer other services as well, such as checking oil and windshield wiper fluid. These employees work for tips, so offer some change as a sign of gratitude for their service.

Most traffic regulations and warnings are represented by internationally recognized symbols and signs, but some signs are unique to Mexico. Traffic must stop completely at *Alto* (halt) signs.

Driving while intoxicated or otherwise under the influence is strictly prohibited *(p129)*, and the city often has drunk driving checkpoints where drivers are obligated to pull over for testing.

In the event of an accident, be sure to follow the procedures established by your rental car company, and contact relevant emergency authorities.

Cycling

Mexico City has more than 140 miles (230 km) of bike lanes, most of which are well-marked and protected from vehicular traffic. Drivers are generally respectful of cyclists, who, along with pedestrians, enjoy the legal right of way, though they are also obliged to follow basic rules of the road. Wearing a helmet is highly recommended.

The city's bike share program, **Ecobici,** covers an extensive part of the city and and is affordable and easy to use. It features nearly 700 stations, with more than 6,500 bikes. The bike share runs from 5am to 12:30am daily and uses the MI card *(p123)*. You can purchase 1-, 3-, or 7-day plans. Day plans are $123 and allow an unlimited number of rides for 45-minutes each.

Ecobici
W ecobici.cdmx.gob.mx

Walking

The most rewarding way to get around the city and savor local life is on foot. Though Mexico City is sprawling, many of its most visited neighborhoods – Centro Histórico, Juárez and Cuauhtémoc, and Roma, Condesa, Coyoacán, San Angél, and Polanco – are easily walkable as is Bosque Chapultepec. Most of the city, nestled in a valley surrounded by mountains, is flat, so does not pose strenuous challenges. Be sure to hydrate, due to the high altitude of the city. Most intersections have crosswalks and many have lights for pedestrians as well.

PRACTICAL INFORMATION

A little local know-how goes a long way in Mexico City. On these pages you can find all the essential advice and information you will need to make the most of your trip.

Passports and Visas

For entry requirements, including visas, consult your nearest Mexican embassy or check with the **Mexican Department of Foreign Relations**. All travelers to Mexico need a passport that is valid for six months longer than their intended period of stay.

Citizens of the US, Canada, the UK, Australia, New Zealand, and the Schengen region do not need visas to enter Mexico as tourists for less than 180 days.

Mexican Department of Foreign Relations
W portales.sre.gob.mx/guiadeviaje

Government Advice

Now more than ever, it is important to consult both your and the Mexican government's advice before traveling. The **Gobierno de Mexico**, the **US Department of State**, the UK Foreign, Commonwealth and Development Office (**FCDO**), and the **Australian Department of Foreign Affairs and Trade** offer the latest information on security, health, and local regulations.

Australian Department of Foreign Affairs and Trade
W smartraveller.gov.au
FCDO
W gov.uk/foreign-travel-advice
Gobierno de Mexico
W gob.mex
US Department of State
W state.gov

Customs Information

You can find information on the laws relating to goods and currency taken in or out of Mexico on the Gobierno de Mexico's **Aduanas** website.

Aduanas
W anam.gob.mx/pasajeros

Insurance

We recommend that you take out a comprehensive insurance policy covering theft, loss of belongings, medical care, cancelations, and delays, and read the small print carefully.

Vaccinations

No inoculations are required for visiting Mexico, but all travelers are advised to consider immunization against hepatitis A, typhoid, and tetanus. If you are planning on traveling beyond Mexico City, you should also seek vaccinations against diphtheria, hepatitis B, and rabies.

Money

Most major credit and debit cards are accepted almost everywhere. Contactless payments are increasingly common; however, small businesses, street food stands, and market vendors often prefer cash (or accept it exclusively) and/or charge a fee for paying by credit or debit card. It is always worth carrying some cash for smaller items and tips, and smaller denominations are recommended, as many vendors are unable to make change for large bills. Cash machines can be found at banks.

Money exchanges *(casas de cambio)* are available at the airports and throughout the city, especially along Paseo de la Reforma and in the neighborhoods of Zona Rosa, Roma, Condesa, and Polanco.

Tipping is customary. A tip of 15–20 percent of the total bill is expected in restaurants, and hotel porters and housekeeping will expect a tip of $1 per bag or day; round up taxi fares to the nearest dollar.

Travelers with Specific Requirements

Mexico City can be challenging to navigate for people with physical disabilities; however, a growing number of establishments are making notable efforts to improve accessibility. This is especially true of museums, which provide wheelchair-accessible entrances and restrooms, as well as audio tours. It is best to call historic buildings, hotels, and restaurants in advance to ask about amenities. It is also recommended to check online resources such as the **Accessible Tourism in Mexico City** brochure for detailed advice.

While people with disabilities are able to use the city's public transportation system free of charge, they may find it difficult to do so. Most Metro stations are not easily accessible for people with mobility needs, however, the Metrobús is better equipped, as nearly all stations have priority boarding areas, ramps, and elevators. All other buses in Mexico City are also wheelchair-accessible.

Accessible Tourism in Mexico City
W turismo.cdmx.gob.mx/turismo-accesible

Language

Spanish is the official language spoken in Mexico City. In tourist areas, English is widely spoken, but locals will appreciate efforts to communicate in Spanish.

Opening Hours

Museums are usually open 10am (noon on Sundays) to 5pm; most are closed on Mondays.

Stores open at 10am or 11am and close at 6pm or 7pm Monday to Saturday. On Sundays many shops open late and close early.

On public holidays most places close early or for the day.

The Metro begins at 5am Monday to Saturday and 6am on Sunday, and stops running at midnight daily. The Metrobús runs from 4:30am Monday to Friday and from 5am on Saturday and Sunday. Services stop at midnight daily.

Situations can change quickly and unexpectedly. Always check before visiting attractions and hospitality venues for up-to-date opening hours and booking requirements.

Personal Security

Mexico City is generally safe, but petty crime does take place. Pickpockets work known tourist areas, busy streets, and public transportation. Use your common sense, leave valuables in a hotel safe, avoid wearing flashy jewelry, keep cash concealed, and don't walk with your phone in hand.

If you have anything stolen or experience crime, report the incident as soon as possible to the Mexico City Police Department. Be sure to obtain a copy of the crime report to claim on your insurance. Most Metro and other public transportation stations have uniformed officers visible to the public. Contact your embassy or consulate immediately if your passport is stolen or in the event of a serious crime or accident.

As a rule, Chilangos (residents of Mexico City) are very accepting of all people, regardless of their race, gender, or sexuality. same-sex marriage was legalized in Mexico City in December 2009 and the LGBTQ+ community here is the most prominent in the country. Discrimination on the basis of sexual orientation has been made illegal.

Health

Healthcare in Mexico City, especially at private facilities, is generally excellent; however, medical travel insurance is highly recommended to cover costs related to an accident or sudden illness. Should you be in a serious accident, an ambulance will pick you up and may charge on the spot.

For minor ailments or concerns, most pharmacies have an on-site doctor who can diagnose and treat you, with the pharmacy itself filling most prescriptions. Many pharmacies are open 24 hours.

Smoking, Alcohol, and Drugs

Mexico has become increasingly serious about public health and its link to smoking, and has passed some of the strictest legislation in the world. Smoking and vaping are banned in all public spaces, such as bus and train stations, airports, and in bars, cafés, restaurants, and hotels. Smoking and vaping are also prohibited at beaches, outdoor parks and amusement parks, and historic and archaeological sites, even if they are outdoors. Centro Histórico is an entirely smoke-free

AT A GLANCE

EMERGENCY NUMBERS

GENERAL EMERGENCY

911

TIME ZONE

Mexico City is on Central Standard Time (CST) and does not observe Daylight Saving Time.

TAP WATER

Tap water is not potable and visitors are advised to drink bottled or treated water only.

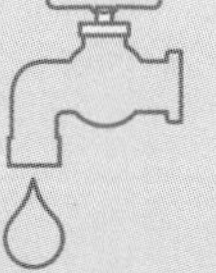

WEBSITES AND APPS

Mexico City website
Official visitor website for Mexico City (*mexicocity.cdmx.gob.mx*), providing plenty of useful tourist information.

Mexico City Metro Map & Route app
This app provides a route map of the Metro and has a journey planner to find the quickest route to your destination.

ECOBICI app
Find bike docking stations near you and receive real-time updates on bike and dock availability using this app.

area, including streets, plazas, parks, and all outdoor areas within the district. While enforcement may not be as robust as the law itself, fines can be stiff for those who run afoul of the law.

Alcohol may not be sold to or bought for anyone under the age of 18. Penalties are severe for those who drink to excess and are caught driving. The legal blood alcohol limit for drivers is 0.04 percent in Mexico City, so it is best to avoid drinking altogether if you plan to drive.

Recreational cannabis use by adults is a complicated matter in Mexico City. While the Mexican Supreme Court ruled in 2021 that it is unconstitutional to ban personal use of cannabis, the legal and licensing procedures for its sale and consumption have still not been fully actualized. Travelers are advised to forego using cannabis.

ID

Passports are required as ID at airports. When traveling by bus within Mexico, police and immigration authorities may board and ask for passports, to ensure that all are in the country legally.

Responsible Travel

Population density and climate change both take their toll on Mexico City, and travelers should do their best to ensure their impact is minimized. Water shortages are a persistent problem, so do your bit by taking quick showers and reusing towels if staying in a hotel.

Mexico City is in a seismically active zone, so be prepared for earthquakes. Ask about specific instructions at your hotel and locate emergency exits.

The city is often congested, with daily traffic jams, so avoid adding to this and help reduce emissions by using alternative means of travel. Mexico City is an easy place to wander on foot or by bike and it also has a great public transportation system.

Where possible support local businesses: purchase souvenirs direct from local artisans and embrace locally and sustainably sourced cuisine.

Be courteous to locals and respect their privacy, don't take photos of individuals without permission.

Cell Phones and Wi-Fi

The city government has installed more than 34,000 free public Wi-Fi hot spots throughout the city. Look for the CDMX-Internet para Todos network to log on. Almost all hotels, motels, and inns offer free Wi-Fi, as do many cafés, bars, restaurants, and public parks.

If you plan to use your cell phone in Mexico City, consult your service provider before arriving to check the cost and coverage of international service. An alternative is to buy a local SIM card from convenience stores like OXXO and Sanborn's department stores.

Postal Services

Mexico City's postal service is run by Correos de México. The main post office is in Palacio Postal *(p88)*, located in Centro Histórico, and is open from 8am to 4pm Monday to Friday and 8am to noon on Saturday. It is recommended that stamped mail is taken direct to the post office, as many mailboxes on the street are not reliable. For international services it is best to use DHL or FedEx.

Taxes and Refunds

Mexico City's sales tax is 16 percent. Visitors can claim a VAT refund; however, be aware that the process can be quite complicated, with minimum per-store purchase thresholds, differing requirements for cash versus credit or debit card purchases, and the need for receipts and physical goods to be presented for inspection.

Discounts

Mexico City offers discounts on many services and admission fees to senior citizens; however, most of these discounts are reserved for Mexicans and are not extended to visitors without residency status. Many museums are free on Sundays.

PLACES TO STAY

Mexico City's accommodations range from luxurious rooms in familiar upscale hotel chains to boutique B&Bs housed in Art Deco mansions. Because the city is so big, deciding where to stay should be based on where you expect to spend most of your time. There is no bad time to visit Mexico City, but keep in mind that accommodation prices tend to be lower mid-week than on weekends. Perhaps surprisingly, the same is also true for holidays, when the capital empties of residents heading to the coast or abroad.

PRICE CATEGORY

Based on one night's stay in high season for a double room, inclusive of service charges and taxes:

$ up to US$70
$$ US$70–150
$$$ over US$150

Centro Histórico

Antiguo Molino de San Jerónimo Hotel Boutique

M3 San Jerónimo 33, Colonia Centro antiguomolinosj.com · $$$

Experience history up close at this former colonial-era mill in the heart of Mexico City; the owners can trace their heritage to the last king of Xochicalco. Images from the National Archives, and a library and terrace among its cozy common spaces, add even more character.

Downtown Mexico Hotel

M2 Isabel La Católica 30, Colonia Centro downtownmexico.com · $$$

Located inside a 17th-century mansion that also shares space with the restaurant Azúl Histórico and a number of boutiques, this hotel is a short walk to the Zócalo. A rooftop pool and restaurant are added amenities.

Downtown Beds Hostal

M2 Isabel La Católica 30, Colonia Centro downtownmexico.com · $

Want the Downtown Mexico Hotel experience but without the price tag? This hostel, its sister property, is located in the same building and enjoys the same access and amenities as the hotel, but with more modest rooms – and with more budget-friendly rates.

Casa Pepe

M2 República de Uruguay 86, Colonia Centro casapepe.mx/casa-pepe-cdmx · $

A welcome margarita upon arrival? *¡Sí, por favor!* Casa Pepe has all the usual hostel features – lockers, dorm rooms, common areas, Wi-Fi – plus some totally unexpected ones (think in-house concerts and tequila tastings). There's something for everyone, with more than 50 free activities each week.

Hotel Zócalo Central

M2 Av. 5 de Mayo 61, Colonia Centro centralhoteles.com · $$$

If you want to be in the heart of the action, there's no better place; set in a historic building, this hotel overlooks the Zócalo and Catedral Metropolitana. Its rooftop restaurant, with unmatched views, is extremely popular. A gym, steam room, and bike loan program are among the amenities.

Gran Hotel Ciudad de México

M2 16 de Septiembre 82, Colonia Centro granhoteldelaciudaddemexico.com.mx · $$$

This hotel, right on the Zócalo, welcomes guests with a staircase that ascends to one of the capital's most beautiful lobbies. The 19th-century building earns its name, especially for its lovely Art Nouveau-style ceiling. A terrace restaurant and bar yield bird's-eye views of the Zócalo and beyond.

Umbral

M2 Calle de Venustiano Carranza 69, Colonia Centro hilton.com · $$$

This Hilton Curio Collection property wins brownie points for its location, but guests may find it hard to even leave: there's an art gallery, rooftop pool and terrace, hanging garden, mini-cinema, and library.

Around Paseo de la Reforma

Casa Pancha

E6 Avenida Mazatlan 190, Colonia Condesa casapancha.com · $

"Condesa" and "budget-friendly" don't often appear in the same sentence; nor "hostel" and "classy." Casa Pancha, with five shared rooms and one private room, is a welcome exception. Expect tasteful Mexican decor in spare but comfy rooms, kitted out with locally made furniture.

St. Regis Mexico City

F3 Paseo de la Reforma 439, Colonia Cuauhtémoc marriott.com · $$$

This soaring skyscraper hotel looks out onto the sweep of Paseo de la Reforma, with unrivaled views of the Diana the Huntress fountain. For the best panoramas head up to the hotel's posh bar, which also features original artwork by surrealist Leonora Carrington.

Four Seasons Mexico City

F3 Paseo de la Reforma 500, Colonia Juárez fourseasons.com/es/mexico · $$$

Only the Ritz-Carlton is closer to the Bosque de Chapultepec than the Four Seasons, though guests enjoy this hotel's luxurious courtyard as much as access to the city's biggest park. Premier rooms feature private terraces, making you forget for a moment that you're in one of the world's busiest cities.

Hotel Carlota

H2 Río Amazonas 73, Colonia Renacimiento hotelcarlota.mx · $$

This hip hotel has a swish "see and be seen" lobby. And in that lobby? A stylish restaurant, bar, and, incredibly, a pool. Rooms are comfortable and quiet, and guests can enjoy the on-site library or borrow bikes to explore the city.

Hotel Parque México

G5 Av. México 133, Colonia Hipódromo parquemexico.mx · $$$

There's lots to love about this award-winning hotel, including its "step-out-the-front-door" proximity to Parque México, a buzzing neighborhood park bordered by cafés and shops. The stunning rooftop terrace, designed to blend into the leafy surroundings, features a bar and restaurant, as well as live music (son Cubano, jazz, and Mexican marimba) several nights a week.

Hotel San Fernando

G5 Iztaccihuatl 54, Colonia Hipódromo bunkhousehotels.com/hotel-san-fernando · $$$

Coral-coloured rooms, soft textiles, and house plants enliven this trendy Condesa hotel, which aims to impart on its guests the CDMX ideal of La Sobremesa – the languorous time after a meal spent enjoying conversation or a coffee. So tuck into the complimentary rooftop breakfast, relax with a drink in the lobby, and soak up the convivial atmosphere.

Red Tree House

G6 Culiacan 6, Colonia Hipódromo theredtreehouse.com · $$

This bed-and-breakfast, just a couple of blocks from Parque México, is renowned for its warm welcome and dedication to connecting travelers, especially in common spaces like the living room and breakfast terrace. The welcoming property attracts repeat visitors, and is tastefully decorated with Mexican textiles and art.

Casa Decu

G6 Culiacan 10, Colonia Hipódromo decuhotels.com/es-mx/casa-decu • $$

If you didn't know this was a hotel, you'd walk right past thinking it's yet another beautiful Art Deco building in the Hipódromo Condesa neighborhood. Inside, you'll find gorgeous tiled floors and small, but light-filled rooms whose views beckon you outside to explore.

Hippodrome Hotel Condesa

G5 Av. México 188, Hipódromo, Cuauhtémoc hotelhippodrome.com • $$$

This Art Deco-era hotel is literal steps from Parque México, and enjoys a quiet location on a street that is also home to several restaurants and relaxed bars with indoor and outdoor dining. Every room has a Nespresso coffee machine and guests are able to use a nearby gym if they want to exercise.

Colima 71

J4 Colima 71, Colonia Roma Norte colima71.com • $$$

This "art hotel" surged in popularity in 2024 when it exhibited the Chavis Marmól work *Tesla Crushed by an Olmec Head*, a giant stone head dropped on a Tesla. "Working booths" attract artists who want to work – until they're tempted to explore the hip Roma Norte neighborhood that awaits outside.

Casa Cuenca

F4 Cuernavaca 4, Colonia Condesa casacuenca.mx • $$

Ten elegant rooms are available in this 1930s-era home in the popular Condesa neighborhood. An Ecobici station just outside provides easy access to the area's popular restaurants, cafes, and attractions.

VOLGA

G3 Río Volga 105, Colonia Cuauhtémoc hotelvolga.mx • $$$

This hotel sells itself as an "immersive sensory experience," which it delivers through art exhibits, mixology classes and refined Japanese food. The rooftop features a "swimming channel" (think slim pool) and live DJ sets.

Chapultepec and Polanco

Las Alcobas

B2 Av. Presidente Masaryk 390, Polanco marriott.com• $$$

This swanky Marriott Luxury Collection Hotel is located in the heart of tony Polanco, steps from Mexico City's loftiest high-end shops and restaurants. An adults-only property, it features patented "Sterile Aire" ventilation systems, nightly shoe-shining services, and luxury dining.

JW Marriott Hotel Mexico City

C3 Andrés Bello 29, Polanco marriott.com • $$$

This ultimate-luxury hotel has it all: one rooftop pool, five bars, dining experiences, and free transportation to and from the local helipad – if that's how you like to get about. All of its 314 rooms are pet friendly, so in the unlikely event your furry loved one is joining you on vacation in Mexico City, you'll know hey're being well looked after while you enjoy the spa, private mezcal tastings, and concierge-arranged tours and experiences.

W Mexico City

C3 Campos Elíseos 252, Polanco marriott.com • $$$

Over 230 contemporary rooms await at this party-friendly hotel in Polanco, where the lobby pulses with music and good vibes and there's a restorative spa for the morning after the night before. Top-ranked restaurants like Pujol and Quintonil *(p105)* are within walking distance.

Alexander

B5 Bosque de Chapultepec, Pedregal 24 alexanderhotel.mx • $$$

If you want to stay in a work of architectural grandeur, this is the spot. Located in El Dorito, the hotel features custom-designed furniture from

Italy and has its own photography collection. If you're feeling flush, you can dine at the in-house Caviar Bar.

The Wild Oscar

D2 Lamartine 516, Polanco thewildoscar.mx · $$$

Designed for the "educated business voyager" – think dark wood, brass fixtures, and rich leather armchairs – this upscale boutique hotel offers a 360-degree view from its rooftop bar, exclusive for guests. A coworking space, fitness center, and wine bar round out the amenities here.

Camino Real Polanco

E3 Calzada General Mariano Escobedo 700, Colonia Anzures caminoreal.com/caminoreal/camino-real-polanco-mexico · $$$

Designed by architect Ricardo Legorreta for the 1968 Olympics, this classic five-star hotel takes home the gold for its blend of beauty and function. Enjoy artwork by Mexican masters, a hotel pool, and easy access to the Bosque de Chapultepec.

Flow Suites Polanco

C3 Av. Emilio Castelar 34, Polanco flowsuites.com · $$

Ritzy Polanco doesn't have many budget stays, but this place is as close as it gets. Take the pesos you've saved on the room – which includes ample workspace and a kitchenette – and treat yourself to a meal at one of the many world-class restaurants nearby.

Hotel Park Villa

E5 Calle General Gómez Pedraza 68, Colonia San Miguel Chapultepec park-villa.hotels-mexico-city.com · $$

This unassuming hotel, tucked onto a quiet side street in the San Miguel Chapultepec neighborhood, may seem a bit old-fashioned, with its carpeted floors and stenciled flowers painted over beds, but its price and location are hard to beat. This is an ideal landing spot for visitors who want to spend lots of time in the neighborhood's art galleries or in Bosque de Chapultepec, which is a five-minute walk from the hotel's front door.

Coyoacán and San Ángel

Tonalli

U2 Vallarta 7, La Concepción, Coyoacán tonallicasaboutique.mydirectstay.com · $$

Simple but welcoming, this boutique hotel offers comfort and convenience to its guests. It enjoys a prime location for exploring the worlds of Frida Kahlo and Diego Rivera at key sites like Caza Azul and Museo Anahuacallí.

Ágata

T2 Av. México 21, Del Carmen, Coyoacán agatahotelboutiquespa.com · $$

This boutique hotel is a calm retreat from the energy of central Mexico City. Take advantage of the free breakfast, make use of the hotel library (and download a book on their Kindle if you can't find what you're looking for), and enjoy yoga classes, and a spa.

H21 Hospedaje Boutique

U2 Higuera 21, La Concepción, Coyoacán h21.mx · $$$

Nestled in the heart of Coyoacán is a hotel that boasts many virtues, its rooms, named Kindness, Respect, Loyalty, and Patience, for one. It's perfectly positioned for all the key neighborhood attractions nearby.

Greater Mexico City

El Patio 77

H1 Joaquín García Icazbalceta 77, Colonia San Rafael elpatio77.com · $$

This economical B&B is a charming option; each of the eight rooms is decorated in the style of a specific state of Mexico. Delicious breakfasts await each morning, and the friendly care of the owners is a highlight, as is their eco-awareness: the building captures rainwater and has graywater reuse.

INDEX

Page numbers in **bold** refer to main entries

PHRASE BOOK

In an Emergency

Help!	¡Socorro!	*soh-**koh**-roh*
Call a doctor!	¡Llame a un médico!	***yah**-meh ah **oon** **meh**-dee-koh*
Call an ambulance!	¡Llame una ambulancia!	***yah**-meh ah **oonah** ahm-boo-**lahn**-see-ah*
Call the fire department!	¡Llame a los bomberos!	***yah**-meh ah lohs bohm-**beh**-rohs*
police officer	el policía	*ehl poh-lee-**see**-ah*

Communication Essentials

Yes	Sí	*see*
No	No	*noh*
Please	Por favor	*pohr fah-**vohr***
Thank you	Gracias	***grah**-see-ahs*
Excuse me	Perdóne	*pehr-**doh**-neh*
Hello	Hola	***oh**-lah*
Bye (casual)	Chau	*chau*
Goodbye	Adiós	*ah-dee-**ohs***
What?	¿Qué?	***keh***
When?	¿Cuándo?	***kwahn**-doh*
Why?	¿Por qué?	*pohr-**keh***
Where?	¿Dónde?	***dohn**-deh*
How are you?	¿Cómo está usted?	***koh**-moh ehs-**tah** oos-**tehd***
Very well, thank you	Muy bien, gracias	*mwee bee-**ehn** **grah**-see-ahs*
I'm sorry	Lo siento	*loh see-**ehn**-toh*

Useful Phrases

Where is/are…?	¿Dónde está/están…?	***dohn**-deh ehs-**tah**/ehs-**tahn***
How far is it to…?	¿Cuántos metros/ kilómetros hay de aquí a…?	***kwahn**-tohs **meh**-trohs/kee-**loh**-meh-trohs **eye** deh ah-**kee** ah*
Which way is it to…?	¿Por dónde se va a…?	*pohr **dohn**-deh seh **vah** ah*
Do you speak English?	¿Habla inglés?	***ah**-blah een-**glehs***
I don't understand	No comprendo	*noh kohm-**prehn**-doh*
I would like	Quisiera/ Me gustaría	*kee-see-**yehr**-ah meh goo-stah-**ree** ah*

Useful Words

big	grande	***grahn**-deh*
small	pequeño/a	*peh-**keh**-nyoh/nyah*
hot	caliente	*kah-lee-**ehn**-teh*
cold	frío/a	***free**-oh/ah*
good	bueno/a	***bweh**-noh/nah*
bad	malo/a	***mah**-loh/lah*
open	abierto/a	*ah-bee-**ehr**- toh/tah*
closed	cerrado/a	*sehr-**rah**-doh/dah*
left	izquierda	*ees-key-**ehr**-dah*
right	derecha	*deh-**reh**-chah*
(keep) straight ahead	(siga) derecho	*(**see**-gah) deh-**reh**-choh*
near	cerca	***sehr**-kah*
far	lejos	***leh**-hohs*
more	más	***mahs***
less	menos	***meh**-nohs*
entrance	entrada	*ehn-**trah**-dah*
exit	salida	*sah-**lee**-dah*
elevator	el ascensor	***ehl** ah-sehn-**sohr***
toilets	baños/sanitarios	***bah**-nyohs/sah-nee-**tah**-ree-ohs*

Post Offices and Banks

Where can I change money?	¿Dónde puedo cambiar dinero?	***dohn**-deh **pweh**-doh kahm-bee-**ahr** dee-**neh**-roh*
How much is the postage to…?	¿Cuánto cuesta enviar una carta a…?	***kwahn**-toh **kweh**-stah ehn-vee-**yahr** **oo**-nah **kahr**-tah ah*
I need stamps	Necesito estampillas	*neh-seh-**see**-toh ehs-tahm -**pee**-yahs*

Shopping

How much does this cost?	¿Cuánto cuesta esto?	***kwahn**-toh **kwehs**-tah **ehs**-toh*
I would like…	Me gustaría…	*meh goos-tah-**ree**-ah*
Do you have?	¿Tienen?	*tee-**yeh**-nehn*
Do you take credit cards	¿Aceptan tarjetas de crédito	*ahk-**sehp**-tahn tahr-**heh**-tahs deh **kreh**-dee-toh*
expensive	caro	***kahr**-oh*
cheap	barato	*bah-**rah**-toh*
white	blanco	***blahn**-koh*
black	negro	***neh**-groh*
red	rojo	***roh**-hoh*
yellow	amarillo	*ah-mah-**ree**-yoh*
green	verde	***vehr**-deh*
blue	azul	*ah-**sool***
bank	el banco	*ehl **bahn**-koh*
bookstore	la libería	*lah lee-breh-**ree**-ah*
market	el tianguis/ mercado	*ehl tee-ahn-goo-ees/mehr-**kah**-doh*
post office	la oficina de correos	*lah oh-fee-**see**-nah deh kohr-**reh**-ohs*
supermarket	el supermercado	*ehl soo-pehr-mehr-**kah**-doh*
travel agency	la agencia de viajes	*lah ah-**hehn**-see-ah deh vee-**ah**-hehs*

Transportation

When does the…leave?	¿A qué hora sale el…?	*ah **keh** **oh**-rah **sah**-leh ehl*
Where is the bus stop?	¿Dónde está la parada de autobuses?	***dohn**-deh ehs-**tah** lah pah-**rah**-dah deh ow-toh-**boo**-sehs*
Is there a bus/ train to…?	¿Hay un camión/ tren a…?	***eye oon** kah-mee-**ohn**/**trehn** ah tren a…?*
ticket office	la taquilla	*lah tah-**kee**-yah*
round-trip ticket	un boleto de ida y vuelta	***oon** boh-**leh**-toh deh **ee**-dah ee voo-**ehl**-tah*
one-way ticket	un boleto de ida solamente	***oon** boh-**leh**-toh deh **ee**-dah soh-lah-**mehn**-teh*
airport	el aeropuerto	*ehl ah-ehr-oh-poo-**ehr**-toh*
taxi stand/rank	sitio de taxis	***see**-tee-oh deh **tahk**-sees*

Sightseeing

cathedral	la catedral	lah kah-teh- **drahl**
church	la iglesia/ la basílica	lah ee-**gleh**-see-ah/ lah bah-**see**-lee-kah
garden	el jardín	ehl hahr-**deen**
museum	el museo	ehl moo-**seh**-oh
pyramid	la pirámide	lah pee-**rah**-meed
tourist information office	la oficina de turismo	lah oh-fee-**see**-nah deh too-**rees**-moh
ticket	la entrada	lah ehn-**trah**-dah
guide (person)	el/la guía	ehl/lah **gee**-ah
guide (book)	la guía	lah **gee**-ah
map	el mapa	ehl **mah**-pah

Staying in a Hotel

Do you have a vacant room?	¿Tienen una habitación libre?	tee-**eh**-nehn **oo**-nah ah-bee-tah-see-**ohn lee**-breh
double room	habitación doble	ah-bee-tah-see-**ohn doh**-bleh
single room	habitación sencilla	ah-bee-tah-see-**ohn** sehn-**see**-yah
room with a bath/ shower	habitación con baño la ducha	ah-bee-tah-see-**ohn** kohn **bah**-nyoh lah **doo**-chah
I have a reservation	Tengo una habitación reservada	tehn-goh **oo**-nah ah-bee-tah-see-**ohn** reh-sehr-**vah**-dah
key	la llave	lah**yah**-veh

Eating Out

Have you got a table for…	¿Tienen una mesa para…?	tee-**eh**-nehn **oo**-nah meh-sahpah-**rah**
I want to reserve a table	Quiero reservar una mesa	kee-eh-roh reh-sehr-**vahr** **oo**-nah **meh**-sah
The bill, please	La cuenta, por favor	lah **kwehn**-tah pohr fah-**vohr**
I am a vegetarian	Soy vegetariano/a	soy veh-heh-tah-ree-**ah**-no/na
I am a vegan	Soy vegano/a	soy veh-**gah**-no/na
waiter/waitress	mesero/a	meh-**seh**-roh/rah
menu	la carta	lah **kahr**-tah
wine list	la carta de vinos	lah **kahr**-tah deh **vee**-nohs
glass	un vaso	**oon vah**-soh
knife	un cuchillo	**oon** koo-**chee**-yoh
fork	un tenedor	**oon** teh-neh-**dohr**
spoon	una cuchara	**oo**-nah koo-**chah**-rah
breakfast	el desayuno	ehl deh-sah-**yoo**-noh
lunch	la comida	lah koh-**mee**-dah
dinner	la cena	lah **seh**-nah
main course	el plato fuerte	ehl **plah**-toh foo-**ehr**-teh
starters	las entradas	lahs ehn-**trah**-das

Menu Decoder

el aceite	ah-**see**-eh-teh	oil
las aceitunas	ah-seh-**toon**-ahs	olives
el agua mineral	**ah**-gwa mee-neh-**rahl**	mineral water
el ajo	**ah**-hoh	garlic
el arroz	ahr-**rohs**	rice
el azúcar	ah-**soo**-kahr	sugar
una bebida	beh-**bee**-dah	drink
el café	kah-**feh**	coffee
la carne	**kahr**-neh	meat
la cebolla	seh-**boh**-yah	onion
la cerveza	sehr-**veh**-sah	beer
el cerdo	**sehr**-doh	pork
el chocolate	choh-koh-**lah**-teh	chocolate
la ensalada	ehn-sah-**lah**-dah	salad
la fruta	**froo**-tah	fruit
el helado	eh-**lah**-doh	ice cream
el huevo	oo-**eh**-voh	egg
el jugo	ehl **hoo**-goh	juice
la langosta	lahn-**gohs**-tah	lobster
la leche	**leh**-cheh	milk
la mantequilla	mahn-teh-**kee**-yah	butter
los mariscos	mah-**rees**-kohs	seafood
el pan	**pahn**	bread
el pescado	pehs-**kah**-doh	fish
picante	pee-**kahn**-teh	spicy
la pimienta	pee-mee-**yehn**-tah	pepper
el pollo	poh-yoh	chicken
el postre	**pohs**-treh	dessert
el queso	**keh**-soh	cheese
el refresco	reh-**frehs**-koh	soft drink/soda
la sal	**sahl**	salt
la salsa	**sahl**-sah	sauce
la sopa	**soh**-pah	soup
el té	**teh**	herb tea (usually camomile)
el té negro	**teh neh**-groh	tea
la torta	**tohr**-tah	sandwich
las tostadas	tohs-**tah**-dahs	toast
el vinagre	vee-**nah**-greh	vinegar
el vino blanco	**vee**-noh **blahn**-koh	white wine
el vino tinto	**vee**-noh **teen**-toh	red wine

Numbers

0	cero	**seh**-roh
1	uno	**oo**-noh
2	dos	dohs
3	tres	trehs
4	cuatro	**kwa**-troh
5	cinco	**seen**-koh
6	seis	says
7	siete	**see**-eh-teh
8	ocho	**oh**-choh
9	nueve	**nweh**-veh
10	diez	dee-**ehs**
20	veinte	**veh**-een-teh
30	treinta	**treh**-een-tah
40	cuarenta	kwah-**rehn**-tah
50	cincuenta	seen-**kwehn**-tah
60	sesenta	seh-**sehn**-tah
70	setenta	seh-**tehn**-tah
80	ochenta	oh-**chehn**-tah
90	noventa	noh-**vehn**-tah
100	cien	see-**ehn**
200	doscientos	dohs-see-**ehn**- tohs
500	quinientos	khee-nee-**ehn**-tohs
1,000	mil	meel

Time

one minute	un minuto	**oon** mee-**noo**-toh
one hour	una hora	**oo**-nah **oh**-rah
half an hour	media hora	**meh**-dee-ah **oh**-rah
Monday	lunes	**loo**-nehs
Tuesday	martes	**mahr**-tehs
Wednesday	miércoles	mee-**ehr**-koh-lehs
Thursday	jueves	hoo-**weh**-vehs
Friday	viernes	vee-**ehr**-nehs
Saturday	sábado	**sah**-bah-doh
Sunday	domingo	doh-**meen**-goh

ACKNOWLEDGMENTS

This edition updated by

Contributor Julie Schwietert Collazo

Sensitivity Reader Jan de la Rosa

Senior Editor Alison McGill

Senior Designers Laura O'Brien, Vinita Venugopal

Project Editors Keith Drew, Anuroop Sanwalia

Project Art Editor Tanvi Sahu

Editors Charlie Baker, Nandini Desiraju, Tavleen Kaur, Anjasi N.N.

Proofreaders Kathryn Glendenning, Ben Ffrancon Dowds

Indexer Vanessa Bird

Picture Research team Virien Chopra, Nishwan Rasool, Samrajkumar S, Priya Singh

Publishing Assistant Simona Velikova

Jacket Designer Laura O'Brien

Jacket Picture Researcher Claire Guest

Senior Cartographers Subhashree Bharati, James Macdonald

Cartography Manager Suresh Kumar

Senior DTP Designer Tanveer Zaidi

DTP Designers Nand Kishor Acharya, Neeraj Bhatia, Rohit Rojal, Vikram Singh

Pre-production Manager Balwant Singh

Image Retouching-Production Manager Pankaj Sharma

Production Controller Kariss Ainsworth

Managing Editors Beverly Smart, Hollie Teague

Managing Art Editor Gemma Doyle

Senior Managing Art Editor Priyanka Thakur

Art Director Maxine Pedliham

Publishing Director Georgina Dee

DK would like to thank the following for their contribution to the previous editions: Nancy Mikula

The publisher would like to thank the following for their kind permission to reproduce their photographs:

Key: a-above; b-below/bottom; c-center; f-far; l-left; r-right; t-top

Alamy Stock Photo: Amanda Ahn 55t; Album 25tl; Associated Press / Alexandre Meneghini 11t; Arpad Benedek 94–95tc; Cavan Images 70–7; Marcia Chambers 72t; David Crossland 42–43t; directphoto.bz 60br, 110b; Diversbelow 58tl; Richard Ellis 66t; Eyepix Group / Ian Robles 10bl; Guiziou Franck 75br; Geogphotos 15tr, 64–65t; GlowImages / PantherMedia 12cr; Scott Goodno 21cl, 39b; Jeremy Graham 107tr; Granger - Historical Picture Archive 9cra; Lindsay Lauckner Gundlock 97tr; Andrew Hasson 43crb; Hemis / Nicolas José 23tr; imageBROKER.com GmbH & Co. KG / Egon Boemsch 13cl; Leandro Izaguirre 40cra; Japhotos 13cla; Jeffrey Isaac Greenberg 10+ 119tl; Jeffrey Isaac Greenberg 12+ 13clb; Jeffrey Isaac Greenberg 5+ 109bl; Jeffrey Isaac Greenberg 8+ 96bl; Madeleine Jettre 35tr; JJM Stock Photography 44bl; Inge Johnsson 60bl; Jon Arnold Images Ltd / John Coletti 51; JSM Historical 8b; Bjanka Kadic 108t; Kari 94bl; Christian Kober 1 12br; Frans Lemmens 91br; Chon Kit Leong 30b; Loop Images Ltd / Tom Hanslien 73bl; Cathyrose Melloan 16cra; John Mitchell 26cb; MJ Photography 36br; NDK 31cr; Frank Nowikowski 21cra; Brian Overcast 29tr; 38tl, 47tc, 62tr, 83; David Parker 77tl; PJPhoto 60–61t; Prisma Archivo 9tl; Realy Easy Star 10tl; Marko Reimann 103tl; Anne Rippy 48t; Robertharding / Tony Waltham 28b; M. Sobreira 24bl, 26bl; Lucas Vallecillos 88bl, 90t; Little Valleys 25b.

AWL Images: Marco Bottigelli 1; John Coletti 27t.

Depositphotos Inc: Bruno135 43br; DmitryRukhlenko 46–47b; Eduardo1304 81t; Richie0703 59t.

Dreamstime.com: Albertoloyo 80br; Andreistanescu 78–79bc; Carlos Araujo 76b; Oksana Byelikova 13bl; Coralimages2020 59bc; Elovkoff 112–113t; Daniel Gomez 67bl; Diego Grandi 13cl (8); Izanbar 26br; Kmiragaya 32–33t; 39tc, 113br; Chon Kit Leong 86–87b, 104t; Arlette Lopez 16cl; Marketa Novakova 12cra, 16tl, 17b, 22b, 116t, 118b; Oasisamuel 36–37t; William Perry 14bl, 85tr; Photosimo 15br; Massimiliano Rastello 19, 43bl; Witold Ryka 31tl, 115bl; Sl Photography 73tr; Aleksandar Todorovic 13tl; Евгений Вершинин 12crb.

Getty Images: Archive Photos / Kean Collection 9br; Bettmann 65br; Corbis Historical / Nik Wheeler 10br; De Agostini / Dea / G. Dagli Orti 9tr; © Fitopardo 26clb; LatinContent WO / Hector Vivas / Stringer 69tl; Medios y Media 78tl; Popperfoto / Ed Lacey 10cla; Stone / Edgardo Contreras 41b; The Image Bank / John Coletti 54bl; The Washington Post 105br; Universal Images Group / Jeff Greenberg 101tr.

Getty Images / iStock: Apomares 21tl; Benedek 56b; Marco Antonio Blanco 113bl; Rui Mesquita Cordeiro 43cb; E+ / GMVozd 74bl; E+ / Orbon Alija 21bc, 49br; Elaine Den Enting 68bl; Mattgush 5; Eve Orea 52b; Redtea 15bc; Starcevic 6–7; Itza Villavicencio Urbieta 53tl.

OXA: 111tl.

Shutterstock.com: Aberu.Go 98–99; Marcos Castillo 121; Elena Diego 57tl; FCHM 93tl; Yenny Grajales 45t; Marianna Ianovska 20crb; ItzaVU 102b; Nekomura 15clb, 63tr, 89tr; R.M. Nunes 34–35bc; E Pasqualli 33bl; Guadalupe Polito 16tc.

Cover Images:

Front and Spine: **Getty Images:** Sergio Mendoza Hochmann; *Back:* **Alamy Stock Photo:** David Crossland tr; **Depositphotos Inc:** DmitryRukhlenko tl; **Getty Images / iStock:** Mattgush cl.

Sheet Map Cover Image:

Getty Images: Sergio Mendoza Hochmann.

A NOTE FROM DK

The rate at which the world is changing is constantly keeping the DK travel team on our toes. While we've worked hard to ensure that this edition of Mexico City is accurate and up-to-date, we know that opening hours alter, standards shift, prices fluctuate, places close and new ones pop up in their stead. So, if you notice we've got something wrong or left something out, we want to hear about it. Please get in touch at travelguides@dk.com

Within each Top 10 list in this book, no hierarchy of quality or popularity is implied. All 10 are, in the editor's opinion, of roughly equal merit.

First edition 2008

Published in Great Britain by Dorling Kindersley Limited,
DK, One Embassy Gardens, 8 Viaduct Gardens,
London SW11 7BW, UK

The authorised representative in the EEA is
Dorling Kindersley Verlag GmbH. Arnulfstr.
124, 80636 Munich, Germany

Published in the United States by DK Publishing,
1745 Broadway, 20th Floor, New York, NY 10019, USA

24 25 26 27 10 9 8 7 6 5 4 3 2 1

A CIP catalog record for this book
is available from the British Library.

A catalog record for this book is available
from the Library of Congress.

ISSN: 1542 1554
ISBN: 978 0 2416 9810 5

Printed and bound in China

www.dk.com

MIX
Paper | Supporting responsible forestry
FSC™ C018179

This book was made with Forest Stewardship Council™ certified paper – one small step in DK's commitment to a sustainable future.

Learn more at **www.dk.com/uk/information/sustainability**